MINISTRY WITH THE DIVORCED

Ministry with the Divorced

Peter R. Monkres

The Pilgrim Press
New York

The scripture quotations in this book are from the *Revised Standard Version of the Bible,* copyright 1946, 1952 and © 1971 and 1973 by the Division of Christian Education, National Council of Churches, and are used by permission. The excerpts in chapter two from Joseph E. Kerns, *The Theology of Marriage: The Historical Development of Christian Attitudes Toward Sex & Sanctity in Marriage,* are copyright 1964 Sheed & Ward, Inc. Reprinted with permission of Andrews, McMeel & Parker. All rights reserved.

Library of Congress Cataloging-in-Publication Data

Monkres, Peter R., 1946–
  Ministry with the divorced.

  1. Divorce—Religious aspects—Christianity.
2. Church work with divorced people. I. Title.
BT107.M66   1985   261.8'3589   85-12338
ISBN 0-8298-0566-4

The Pilgrim Press, 132 West 31 Street, New York, NY 10001

Contents

Introduction

When I began the research for this book, I wondered whether it would be possible to acquire enough first-person accounts of the volatile experience of divorce to make credible observations. True, I had suffered through a divorce in my early twenties and felt prepared to reflect on my own experiences. I worried, however, about the willingness of strangers to share their pain and hurt with me.

Thus I came face to face with my own shyness in asking people I did not know to share intimate feelings with me. In the early stages of the project I fantasized that my questionnaire would seem a burden and that many would perceive me as an entrepreneur of tragedy.

With such anxieties stalking the project, I sent out a questionnaire. My first thought was to produce a data base with statistical validity. I planned to quantify data, document emotions, and otherwise verify the experiences of the divorced in the best sociological manner. As I allowed these initial impressions to ripen, I thought better of my plan. I came to realize that the honest impact of people's stories might be more valuable than statistical study.

I decided, therefore, to ask questions that would allow divorced men and women to have their say in an emotive way. Five areas of inquiry that would address essential concerns in the lives of divorced and divorcing Christians were posed. The specific questions read:

1. Please share the major emotions, feelings, and images that came to you in the midst of divorce. How long did working your way through this experience take? Which transitions were the most difficult and which seemed most resolvable?
2. What were your major sources of support in working your way through the experience of divorce? Please mention both people and institutions that were helpful to you, and describe the kind of support they offered.
3. What sources of support did you feel were absent during divorce? Were there places and people that you sought out for support and found unresponsive?
4. What part did your Christian faith play during your divorce? Was faith a healing resource? Did faith seem dry or disappointing because of divorce? Which aspects of Christian faith encouraged you most? Which were least helpful?
5. What part did your church play during your divorce? What messages were communicated to you by the liturgy (prayer, scripture, sermon, eucharist, hymns), the other members of the church, and the pastor?

The response to these questions humbled me. I received more than ninety replies, and those who responded spoke from the heart.

As I read through the stories I received I was struck by their deep sense of honesty. Many shared confidential information with me. Others ached and cried through their words. Gradually, a collective voice of the divorced spoke and gave the following testimony.

First, and most poignant, is the pain of the divorced. As chapter 1 demonstrates, divorce is a hurtful experience that sends people into loneliness and despair. Second, paradoxical feelings of freedom occur during divorce. As painful as the experience is, the breaking of marriage vows also involves feelings of expectation and hope for a new life.

Third, friendships are essential in the healing process.

Those who have been healed from divorce most decisively are those who were gifted with compassionate and understanding relationships.

Fourth, faith plays an essential role in the lives of divorcing Christians. Those who responded to the questionnaire consistently commented on their relationship with God and with faith resources, such as prayer and scriptural study, with great intensity. Their relationships were not always smooth. Many responders spoke of anger at God and of the dryness of their faith. However, this exiled state was counterpointed by moments of release and transcendence. The stories speak of God as a companion through the valley of the shadow of death, who keeps company with them through deepening grief until, gradually, the loss of a marriage is overcome by time and a new level of faith is reached.

Finally, those who responded to the questionnaire shared an ambiguous impression of the church's ministry to the divorced. In many cases this ministry was helpful and healing. Yet there are significant undercurrents that make the church's practice of compassionate ministry with the divorced tentative. The stories make it clear that the church needs attitudinal changes in order to deepen its relationship with those who suffer from broken marriages.

All stories are anonymous. Many men and women who responded to the questionnaire asked that their sharing be held in confidence, and I have honored this request.

Is there a difference between the ways that men and women share their experiences? Yes. The stories document many theories that have arisen in feminist and psychological circles in recent years. They suggest that, in general, women are much clearer about and more aware of the process of soul-searching.

The women who responded to my questionnaire painted the pages with emotions and feelings. They journeyed deep within themselves and shared freely from their storehouse of experiences. Thus the stories of women were more candid.

They cried through their pens when describing the pain of their divorces and named their healing with laughter. Women do not move through divorce easily. There is great suffering. Yet there is, in women's stories, a gracious ability to move through the inner labyrinths, to name what is there honestly, and to avoid the temptation to glamorize. Women soul-search as water flows around rocks, and their inner accounts refresh one like a cool drink from a mountain stream.

I received many wonderful stories from men as well. Some were deeply sensitive and insightful. Yet the stories of men were more inconsistent. If women search the soul like flowing water, men are the miners of the psyche. Men clearly intuit that the inner realm is a place of riches but as a gender have not yet developed the art of soul-searching. Where women surrender to their feeling state, men battle it. Where women commune with the feelings that accompany the loss of a love, men seek to conquer them and to return to a pain-free state as quickly as possible. As a result, the stories of men were generally less detailed and expressed frustration over the emotional turmoil that had taken center stage in their lives.

It is my hope that men will grow in their ability to soften their relationship with their own emotional and spiritual universe so that they can coexist with pain, despair, and loss in more sensitive ways. There is a profound need for the church to teach about men's reality, including most especially friendships and the art of the inner journey. I also hope that opportunities in this area will evolve and provide an alternative to the epidemic state of loneliness among men.

I received many kind notes from those who returned the questionnaire. To my surprise, I discovered that, for many people, writing about divorce was a healing exercise:

> Thank you so much for giving me the opportunity to share my story. It helped me to put more things into perspective concerning my divorce. It was therapeutic for me.

* * *

I must admit that getting this letter was like having alcohol poured on an open wound. I don't like being reminded of the past, and yet at the same time it seems so good to talk to someone. Thanks.

I am deeply appreciative of those who have shared their loves and lives with me. I hope that I have managed to reflect the reality of their experiences and to draw from them implications that will encourage the church to deepen its healing ministry with the divorced.

MINISTRY WITH THE DIVORCED

CHAPTER ONE

Of Death and Flights of Freedom

Our understanding of divorce begins when we focus on the lives of those who have experienced it. When we hear their stories and empathize with the reality of their emotions, we discover that divorce has far less to do with sin or moral failure than with grief. The most central characteristic of divorce is that it marks people with a death in their lives. And, like any person experiencing the loss of a love, a divorced man or woman needs compassion and the gift of a healing ministry in order to work his or her way into new hope.

All divorce is circumscribed by significant emotional pain. Divorce is the pain of a broken heart, of shattered hopes and promises that puncture love like shards of broken glass. It is the pain that comes from the unraveling of a relationship originally founded on great hopes and innocent dreams. Those who experience divorce tell of running a gauntlet of grief, where they are whipped by the fragile reality of a failed relationship in their lives and burdened by guilt over their own inability to sustain it.

Divorce is a separating moment, an act of isolation that leads people from love into loneliness. The word divorce, in fact, comes from the Latin term *divortium*, which means "to turn different ways." When they divorce, a couple that has shared deeply breaks the commitment to seek into the truth pool of each other's eyes. Instead, they turn their backs on each other at a fork in the road and make their way toward separate futures. Divorce is that separating moment when two weary travelers who are tired of carrying the weight of broken dreams decide to go on alone despite the fear and uncertainty that such a journey entails.

Divorced men and women have been described by one writer as "naked nomads." Indeed, the divorced suffer through great emotional exposure during their journey out of marriage. In the first months the nights are filled with memories that whisper of the loved one who has been lost. Beguiling pictures dance in one's mind at the most vulnerable hours. Unbidden and dreaded, a vignette of one's former spouse unfolds in one's fantasies and stirs the grief that lies more comfortably latent during the busy hours of the day. A favorite restaurant, a walk taken during the sweet moments of a marriage, old friends, a well-worn jazz album that filled one's house with music on romantic winter evenings: all the things that subtly represent the meaning of a person's life now conspire to remind him that he is now alone. And there are the fantasies. A wife wonders how her husband is doing and is suddenly filled with the thought that he is joyfully involved in life, never missing a beat, while she suffers from a loss that has crippled and wounded. A husband imagines that his wife is involved in new, fulfilling relationships with other men while he fears to reach out again.

Guilt also plays its part during these lonely moments that follow divorce. In the quiet times one's life seems vulnerable and exposed. There is ample opportunity to face one's frailties and failures, as an insightful woman observed:

At one point whenever I gave love (like a hug to someone in trouble) I would go into a deep depression. I would have images that I was shrinking or that my face had cracked and all my insides leaked out until I was just a pool on the floor. I felt like a failure, unlovable, ugly, that I had no desirable qualities. I hated to be seen alone; I was sure that everyone knew I was a person whom no one loved. I thought my family was broken up and that I had broken it up. I thought I should have been better, that there were answers I should have known and things I should have done. The hardest thing for me to admit (although I knew for years that he was not good for me) was that I wasn't good for him, that he could be happier and more fulfilled alone or with someone else.

Divorce challenges each person to examine her or his shadow side. The experience confronts us with our failures, our limitations, our resentments, our cruelties, and our self-righteousness. We remember the charges that our spouses leveled at us during the inevitable fights that are part of every marriage, and we feel shame about the weak points that they exposed to us: "You always think you're right!" "You think you know everything!" "I'm sick and tired of your bad temper!" During the course of a marriage we may be told that we are stupid, critical, judgmental, aloof, mean, controlling, cold, uncaring, or a number of other things. Such charges often have something of the truth in them, even if they are used in the middle of a marital fight to hurt rather than to offer insight. Consequently, they have a burrlike quality to them and cling to our psyches. After a divorce they begin to scratch and irritate our vulnerable self-image. They cause us to evaluate our own role in a divorce, and this process involves confronting one's failures. Just as divorced people reminisce about the sweet aspects of their marriages, so they are also led to ponder their own equation of personhood, judging particularly their responsibility for the breaking of relationship. A divorced pastor wrote: "What stands out most clearly for me is a sense of failure. Commitments and covenants made were broken. The model of our marriage . . . did not match reality. The hurt caused to others as well as ourselves was very painful."

In our best moments, we as Christians wax poetic about the power of love. Paul, for instance, tells us that love is an indomitable power that "hopes all things, endures all things [1

Cor. 13:7]." The church has spoken definitively of "marriages made in heaven" and has intoned, along with George Bernard Shaw, "What God hath joined together, no man shall put asunder." Such sentiments are true in an idealistic sense. God indeed blesses deep commitment and laughs when lovers lose themselves in each other. There is a uniquely noble and spiritual dimension in marriage, one identified in the ancient book of Genesis, where it is written that "a man leaves his father and his mother and cleaves to his wife, and they become one flesh [2:24]."

It is a mistake, however, to assume that this spiritual dimension of marriage can somehow protect a husband and wife from tragedy or misfortune. Marriages may be made in heaven, but they are surely not maintained there, as any divorced person will quickly testify. As one woman wrote: "God didn't lose sight of me, I now know, but I lost sight of God in significant ways. I felt angry that God should have allowed this to happen to me; it all seemed pointless and unfair."

Marriage is not just a romantic communion; it is also the risk of losing oneself in radical relationship. It is, in a sense, a form of suicide that involves a dying to one's individuality and the discovery of a totally new identity with another. When one discovers that this radical risk is not working, despair is the inevitable outcome. Small wonder, then, that there is such pronounced nervousness between a bride and groom as they exchange their vows. They know, if only intuitively, that they are sacrificing much of their autonomy in order to merge together in shared life.

There can be little doubt that marriage powerfully initiates persons into symbiotic existence, a life that is shaped by shared energies rather than by a mere affiliation of individual desires. Irene Claremont de Castillejo, in her sensitive work *Knowing Woman*, has suggested that a true meeting between

[6]

persons always involves the presence of a "mysterious third."[1] It might be suggested that this mysterious third—the Spirit of love itself—results in the creation of a wholly new hybrid in marriage. This hybrid is, as we have seen, shared identity based on the mutual losing of selves in each other. It is as if a married couple become the warp and woof on a loom on which the mysterious third weaves designs that become the tapestry of marriage.

When divorce occurs a traumatic rending of this tapestry is inevitable. There is much talk these days about amicable divorce with no hard feelings attached. Many books in fact suggest that the ideal of divorce is a separation in which no one has to say that he or she is sorry. But the spiritual nature of marriage makes this kind of divorce impossible, a fact that has too often been ignored in this age of psychological sophistication. In the majority of divorces—even those that are obviously needed—hard feelings and much sorrow occur. Understandably, persons seek for ways to minimize or avoid the suffering that divorce entails, for no one intentionally courts grief. But it is critical to note that such attempts are doomed to failure. The testimonies of divorced people make it clear that grief follows them like a shadow and that steeling oneself to have no regrets does not make the pain of divorce go away. Time and patience, as many have said, are the only true healers. A woman who experienced divorce after a twenty-year marriage writes:

> It took me a full four years to heal after my divorce. Maybe I am a slow healer. Maybe I wasn't as "centered" at the time as some people are. Maybe I am more honest and specific about what I mean by being totally healed. But I think it takes that long for someone who was married as long as I was to begin to establish new traditions, rituals, and habits and make new friends. Maybe it is not so long for shorter marriages, younger people, folks with no children, or people who loved each other

less in the early years. The two people involved go through the stages at different rates and times, causing great suffering to themselves and others around them. And finally, there is a point when both parties recognize the death of the relationship, when the rings come off the fingers and mourning begins with no less pain than the death of a loved one.

It should be suspected that those who champion amicable divorce and comfortable grieving encourage themselves and others to repress the more difficult emotional realities attached to the experience. Such a suspicion should hardly surprise us, because the American life-style emphasizes pain avoidance. Our culture is in fact predicated on the marketing of techniques and tactics for avoiding the specters of death and grief. Any number of writings illustrate this point. Consider Norman Vincent Peale's "power of positive thinking," Robert Schuller's "possibility thinking," and other psychospiritual prescriptions that suggest that an optimistic head can overcome a broken heart. The substance of such approaches can be seen in the following interview with a spiritual teacher:

> When my father died . . . I experienced no sorrow at his passing. If anything, I experienced a tremendous sense of relief and joy. . . . I encouraged my family to grieve only four days for my father because too much grief can bring you down. You can turn a negative thing like death into a positive thing by the way you view it.[2]

Such is our contemporary view of pain. We recognize that pain is a significant teacher and proclaim this fact widely, but we sidestep the implications of the instruction. Again and again, we are seduced by those who promise that loss and death can be waltzed through in a matter of days or weeks merely by having one's "head in the right place." Perhaps. Yet my own experience, as well as the experience of those who responded to the divorce questionnaire, suggests that sorrow

[8]

and sadness exact a steeper price for the lessons they teach than we like to admit. Divorced men and women are rarely creatures who soar above their pain. Their grieving is far more earthy than this and the mystical cure far rarer than the sages of the human potential movement have suggested.

So divorce is like any empty death. It is a loss that chews on the soul, and the suffering always lasts far longer than one wishes. C.S. Lewis managed to capture this feeling in his work *A Grief Observed,* and an insightful woman spoke poignantly of the dimensions of her grief during the early stages of the death of her marriage. Ponder their insights.

> Grief is like a long valley, a winding valley where any bend can reveal a totally new landscape. As I've already noted, not every bend does. Sometimes the surprise is the opposite one; you are presented with exactly the same kind of country you thought you had left behind miles ago. That is when you wonder whether the valley isn't a circular trench.[3]

* * *

> I divorced the only man I have ever loved in my entire life after thirteen years of marriage and three sons. That blind, young love that I thought would see me through everything "for better or worse" was lost so slowly over the years in which we grew further and further apart no matter how hard I tried, and with God as my witness, and a number of other objective observers, I know I really did try.
>
> Now, after three and a half years of being "alone" with my children, the reasons and situations which led to the moment of separation don't really seem important any more. It doesn't matter today what he did to me or I did to him except that it has all finally been digested and stored permanently in my brain for future reference in future relationships, if and when they occur. I can now look back and describe divorce as the most devastating experience a human being can endure. It is death without dying. It is the ultimate rejection, the ultimate failure and defeat, especially if one is raised, as I was, to think

that marriage is a lifetime commitment, a "forever" in God's eyes.

Divorce, then, has never been and can never be a casual separation. Rather, it is a traumatic disruption of the most profound relationship in human experience. Were we to recognize this fact, we should be much more prepared to confront the difficult realities that accompany the death of a marriage. I am not trying to glamorize divorce as a sacred experience; rather, I am suggesting that it is an archetypal one. It is an event that shakes us to the roots of our being, an event that leads us beyond feelings of guilt, worthlessness, and inadequacy. It invites us to fall into despair, as the following story makes clear.

> How can I convey the emotions I felt? I felt emotions I never knew existed. When my husband announced that he didn't love me anymore and wanted a separation, I cried, "Oh, no, no, no!!!" After all the work I had put into our marriage, twenty-six years of doing for him, for our family, and to have it all have been for nothing. The heartache was unbearable. I collapsed, literally. My legs wouldn't hold me. I fell to the floor, my body turned cold, so cold—cold like I had never known before, deep in all my joints, and I thought, "Is this how it feels when people die?" Oh, the shock, the disbelief, the anguish, the feelings of betrayal and pain. I grew numb. Then came the tears, and I fell into a deep depression.

The demons of grief that haunt us after divorce are terribly debilitating. They entice us to capitulate to self-recrimination and freeze our ability to accept the ambiguity of life—in ourselves and in others.

I suffered through a divorce in my early twenties. My first marriage lasted a mere three years. In retrospect, I can see that our relationship was a victim of immaturity, but not an immaturity of the heart. My spouse and I, although young, were not ignorant of the meaning of love. We shared many good times together, and the best of our relationship involved feeding each other's lives and souls. Yet, like many young married couples, we were unprepared to accept imperfection in ourselves and in each other. We swung on a pendulum of love that was eager and sincere but did not have the depth to endure through the crisis points of our lives. Like many young couples, we hoped that our love for each other would help us to find ourselves. Instead, it became all too easy to blame each other for our own tentative qualities of personhood.

Staying power in marriage, I once thought, was a matter of good intentions. I now believe it is a matter of "seasoning," of allowing time spent in relationship to bestow a patina of experience on a relationship whose reach exceeds its grasp. Young couples, for all their yearning for an abiding love, do not always have the deeper knowledge of the rhythm of relationship that allows them to love their way through the ambiguities of their own personhood and their marriage. As a result, the incidence of divorce is high. In retrospect, those who experience divorce in their young adult years come to see that their marriages failed because of their inability to accept imperfection in themselves and in their spouses. In the early stages of divorce this awareness of imperfection fills one with feelings of failure. I recall imagining that my divorce blinked like a seedy neon sign before my friends and family. I felt that to admit I was divorcing was publicly to admit the bankruptcy of my most intimate relationship. Moreover, it was evidence that I had betrayed and hurt another, whom I had promised to cherish and empower. I felt like a phony—a pretender to intimacy who aspires to love another and ends up embracing the air.

One needs time and space to ponder one's emotional injuries as well as one's complicity in a failed marriage. There is no substitute for mourning in loneliness. Much of my healing occurred on a 240-mile backpacking trip through the Sierra

Nevada Mountains of California. Although I enjoyed the company of a friend in the evenings and at rest breaks, I spent most of each day hiking alone. I carried my grief across rocky passes and down winding mountain valleys. I slowly became aware that my pain, like the weight of food in my pack, dropped a little each day. The campfire lit the giant night, a fall blizzard chased me out of the high country for a day, and the alpenglow on the peaks at sunset ate away at my sense of failure. I gradually began to walk lighter.

The times I spent alone during long portions of the day were of irreplaceable value in my healing. These days of solitude gave me the space in which to map the topography of my emotional wilderness. At the same time, the wilderness without taught me that time grinds down grief just as a mountain stream wears down the sharp corners of the stones in its bed. I returned to San Francisco with a capacity to begin again. I had other painful days, of course. I had anxieties about re-involving myself with another woman. I continued to feel some guilt and regret about my divorce and still have experiences and emotions that have not been totally resolved.

A man who participated in the survey shared the persistent feelings of grief that accompanied his divorce:

> Hurt, anger, despondency, guilt, frustration, and maybe after awhile pure numbness. Never a feeling that it was okay. Never a feeling that after a period of time all will work itself out. Time is a healer? How much time? It has been four years now. Sure, life fills gaps, but never are there replacements for the loss. In the same period of time, death took a dear family member. Yet with that pain, it is final. Divorce seems to raise its ugly head to remind you of your failures. There is never a clear-cut separation from that which you loved.

We see, then, that solitude is not a "magic fix" for the pain of divorce. But this is not the critical point. What is at issue is the realization that persons who divorce need a wilderness of silence in which to keep their love and loss in perspective.

The "Range of Light," as John Muir called the Sierras, helped me to focus on my guilt and pain without distraction, gave me space in which to consider that the loss of the greatest love of my life would not permanently disfigure my capacity for relationship, and, finally, led me to see that I had the right to be a whole person despite my inability to sustain a marriage. Solitude, then, is the place in which we are confronted with what one person labeled "that pure panic of loss" that threatens to consume us and are given opportunity to see that we can make it through the fear.

In order to work our way through such feelings, we must learn to coexist with the anxiety that comes from being out of control. As one woman put it:

> There was a real feeling that a part of me was dying and would never be heard from again—the part that was the loving, nurturing, sharing part of a marriage relationship. The fear was of being alone, being unable to cope, being defeated by circumstances.

In her work *Crazy Time,* Abigail Trafford suggests that one must be prepared to wait through several years of uncomfortable, volatile, and paradoxical emotions in order to heal from divorce.

> It starts when you separate and lasts about two years. It's a time when your emotions take on a life of their own and you swing back and forth between wild euphoria and violent anger, ambivalence and deep depression, extreme timidity and rash actions. You are not yourself. Who are you? . . . In all the cocktail party talk about divorce being a growth opportunity for the super new you, nobody tells you about Crazy Time. Yet this is usually the very painful transitions that you have to go through before you can establish a new life for yourself.[4]

Although it is important to wait through "crazy time" in the initial years that follow a divorce, it is also important not to indulge in it. The insightful authors of *The Divorce Book* point out that there are traps that increase the pain of divorce:

[13]

Much of the emotional pain of divorce is inevitable. But some of it is totally unnecessary. Many people increase their pain by falling into cognitive and behavioral traps. Cognitive traps are habitual thoughts that raise your anxiety, depression, and anger like a thermometer in summer. Behavioral traps include a number of classic ways of coping with separation.[5]

Actions that divorced people should avoid are classified by them as follows:

COGNITIVE TRAPS

1. Trying to "read the mind" of others ("They don't like me because I'm divorced.")
2. Generalizing and labeling oneself and others ("My ex-husband is just no damn good.")
3. Overgeneralizing about one's life situation ("Nothing ever works out; I'll always be lonely and I'll never heal from this pain.")
4. Focusing on the worst possible outcome ("This divorce will make it impossible for me to ever trust a woman again.")
5. Self-blame ("If I had been more sensitive, this never would have happened.")
6. Blaming others ("She ruined our marriage by never giving me enough affection.")
7. Worrying about possible outcomes ("What if I can't stand the loneliness and fall apart.")

BEHAVIORAL TRAPS

1. Withdrawal (difficulty in socializing)
2. Dependency on parents or close friends (difficulty in building a new life with new friends)
3. Clinging to an ex-spouse
4. Living for others and ignoring one's own needs
5. Escape from oneself (through drugs, alcohol, eating, work, television)
6. Sexual permissiveness (affairs without intimacy)
7. Rebound relationships (seeking for the perfect partner to fill a lonely life)

[14]

Part of the difficulty in making one's way through the reality of divorce is that of learning to accept its contradictory nature. One must learn to cope not only with the shocks of anger and guilt, but also with the subtle side of grief. If one cannot deal with the full panorama of emotions, one will find oneself ambushed by symbols, memories, and events. We ultimately are forced to move beneath the contradictions of divorce to the pain itself if we want to heal. This pain does not so much come out of the events surrounding the death of a marriage as it does the spaces between them. Moreover, this pain does not come in one terrific impact, but in intermittent waves. Those who responded to the survey on divorce consistently stated that they thought they were through a stage of grieving only to discover it popping up again without warning. As one woman wrote:

> At one time or another I think I experienced every emotion that has ever been experienced. There is the frustration of trying very hard to get beyond certain feelings and emotions only to find yourself in a set of circumstances where you feel you are back at the beginning.

The beginning, of course, is the pain of broken love, the ache that seems both timeless and indelible. One is forced to surrender to it, trusting that it will diminish and accepting that no strategy is capable of eliminating it from one's life.

A pastor who experienced a divorce after twenty-eight years of marriage wrote:

> It was not "the faith" that healed. It was "the faithful" who helped and supported and were encouraged by a very limited and hurting human being whom many trusted, loved, and cared about. I think they knew that I loved and cared, but there was no escape from the pain. I have counseled lots of hurting folk. I have not known any divorce that was without

pain. It was in the pain that I discovered the real meaning of the Christ of the New Testament. We grow up trying to avoid pain. We go to school and become head-trippers about the faith. That's not where it's at when the shit hits the fan. The New Testament has only become real for me since I experienced the pain and discovered my feelings and could talk about them.

The worst of divorce is like "The Fall." It is an eating from the tree of the knowledge of good and evil and an awakening to our separateness. After divorce one no longer remains in an innocent Eden. The pain of divorce is the primal shattering of the innocence of love, for it tells us more than we wanted to know about the ways people can hurt us and the ways that we injure others.

Pain mirrors our complicity in divorce. It leads us to remember the times when we wished our ex-spouse ill or shouted hateful things in a moment of temper. It sets before us an awareness of those moments when we might have turned the relationship around, had we the courage to apologize or initiate a healing possibility. In the same way our pain tells us of our need to release the past. Pius XII once suggested that pain forces people to face "the fundamental question of their fate and to ponder the implications of their pilgrimage on earth." Certainly, this is true in the case of divorce. Our pain is not only a consequence of the intense death of relationships; it is also a result of our estrangement from the way of life we have known. Possessions, traditions, and roots disappear. We must make choices about what shall be taken and what shall be left. We must ponder what it means to "leave the dead to bury their dead." As one woman wrote:

In the past two years I have learned to swallow pride and accept, for a time, welfare to feed my children and keep them warm in the winter months, all the while continuing to work at a full-time job and see to their individual physical, spiritual, and emotional needs as best I can. What it finally comes down to, after going through all the emotions and all the hassles which anger you, but more devastatingly hurt and confuse your children, is that it doesn't matter. You can continue to fight or you can *let go,* and the letting go is the hardest part of divorce. Subconsciously, I think that as long as you are embroiled in a battle, you are still involved with that person you loved and perhaps still do love. When you call a truce, sign a peace treaty in your heart, and *let go* of him in every way, only then can you begin to come out of it. Only then can you look at what you've been through in this process called divorce and put it in perspective, and learn from it.

This releasing of the past or, alternatively, the fight to divide fairly the resources of a marriage that has ended is the cause of much pain. One has already gone through the trauma of the decision to separate and has begun to probe the reasons for the divorce. One has begun to deal with one's anger toward one's spouse for the role that he or she played in the divorce, and one has begun to ponder one's own place in the broken relationship. It is obviously a time of tender feelings, a "Humpty-Dumpty" time when one wonders how one shall ever be put back together again. Just when one feels that one has experienced all the hurt of divorce that there is to share, one is confronted with an unanticipated issue that one is not prepared to handle gracefully. Who shall get what? How do we divide the property fairly? Who owes whom? There are stories about amiable divorce in which people treat one another gracefully and act as the best of friends. Such friends wish one another well, have no hard feelings, and divide the resources of their relationship in generous ways. The mythology involved in such tales is that it is possible to transcend one's ragged emotions and to relate to one's former spouse in a cordial manner. No doubt such a style of relationship is attainable in some cases, but these are the exceptions, not the rule. Far more common are situations in which the division of property becomes the occasion for the resurrection of the problems that led to the divorce in the first place. Divorce does not automatically extinguish the flames of anger, suffering, and pain that accompany an unworkable relationship. Beneath divorce the coals of resentment smolder, and it takes only the briefest stirring to start the blaze anew. The sharing of property and child custody are the two symbols that provide the cause for much stirring. For this reason, discussion of these issues characteristically leads people to feel that they should "stand up for their rights," particularly in situations in which they feel that their spouse has betrayed them or taken unfair advantage of them. A classic example of this kind of situation involves spouses who put their husbands or wives through graduate school programs and then are divorced by them. Such situations are tailor-made for the focusing of grievances through the dividing of property. One feels—sometimes rightly—that one has given more over the years than one's spouse, and one is determined to get her or his fair share out of the relationship. One feels—again with some justification—that one has been abandoned in a capricious or cruel way and focuses on property as a way to get even.

On a pettier level, haggling over possessions creates a situation in which all the old stalemates and deadlocks of the marriage present themselves one last time. A husband visits his wife after separation to clarify child custody and is presented with a list of financial obligations that causes him to rebel in anger. A wife calls her husband and suggests that she deserves to keep the house. He feels it is a product of his creative labors and begins lecturing her about all the ways she has always exploited the relationship for her personal gain. A husband divorces his wife to marry a younger woman and patronizingly informs her of a settlement that takes no notice of her contributions over the years. In all such cases, dramatic or subtle, dividing resources is an occasion for bitterness and anger. A divorced man wrote: "I'm still trying to work that out. . . . I guess I believed that if you treat people decently, they'll reciprocate, and I found out that my ex-wife didn't always play by those rules. Turning the other cheek does not always work—at least in a pragmatic sense."

A clergywoman who was divorced after thirteen years of marriage and who attended seminary only after her marriage ended, pointed out how the division of property can remain a controlling factor in men's and particularly women's lives even after a divorce. She writes:

I followed a very old call, following the divorce, and entered seminary. My ex-husband would have financed any education I sought except theological education, as he could not picture himself as the pastor's husband. . . . We suffered a tremendous financial loss from which we are just now recovering. There were weeks on end when we ate popcorn, oatmeal, and nothing else.

Even when the division of property is less controlling or acrimonious, feelings of insecurity remain about whether or not one will be provided for adequately, either by one's ex-spouse or by oneself. A woman in her midthirties who divorced her husband after he had an affair observed:

Being a woman with two small children and limited income, I would have to say my main concern about divorce was fear of "making it"—whether I could handle the responsibility of single parent alone (financially, emotionally for myself, and physically for my children). I found that being responsible for one's own life is easier than knowing that you have to keep it "together" for your children. . . . But it's a learning experience in a way, and you find that you can make it. You find yourself doing things that you hadn't before—simple tasks like changing a fuse or a tire. After you find that confidence in yourself you can make it. You don't have to rely on anyone for your own personal fulfillment and happiness. You find it in yourself.

Although the loss of one's previous life-style amplifies one's vulnerability, it is not the pivotal event in divorce. Quite clearly, there are more significant issues with which one must contend. What is critical is that divorced people not overlook this dimension of pain, for as we have seen, it needs to be taken into account if one wishes to understand the reality of the feelings that accompany divorce. If these significant symbols that accompany divorce are not reflected on, it is easy to be victimized by them or to underestimate their long-range significance in the lives of the divorced.

When a divorcing couple fights over such symbols no one wins. It is rather like two persons dividing the plunder after a war. The riches gained, if indeed they are realized at all, are icy to the touch. More often than not there is great financial sacrifice on the part of both persons who divorce, as the following story points out:

There was at first a great emptiness. Why go on living? What have I got to live for? I'm just ugly and no good.

Then I began to wonder how I would make a living, how would I pay bills. I didn't want a job; I just wanted to be a farm wife and mother. From August 1978 to January 1980 I pondered these emotions of insecurity. On January 1, the dairy farm was dumped on my shoulders. I am partially disabled from heavy work. I managed the operation as good and, according to the veterinarians, better than my husband. My shoulders and arms started giving me trouble and I sold out in September 1980. I found a part-time housekeeping job that fall. Part-time pay didn't meet my needs so I went to the nursing home. Again, anxiety. That work is heavy. Finally now, in 1984, I had a high evaluation and am feeling better about myself in spite of my painful shoulders. I worry about the debts—the farm mortgage, mainly. It has taken me these four years to just show myself what I am capable of. I just thought that I was totally stupid. My lack of self-confidence really caused me much anxiety. I became very judgmental of my ex-husband and his mother. I still have some bitter feelings. I think they are really harder to resolve than my financial security.

Healing from divorce, it cannot be emphasized too strongly, cannot come from winning property battles or custody fights. It can come only when one resolves the formal concerns of divorce so that the pain can be dealt with directly rather than symbolically.

The battle for child custody can be both more and less painful than the battle that accompanies the dividing of property. Often parents are more sensitive about the issue of custody because they want to be fair to the children. There is, in every divorce involving children, a desire to spare them pain. For this reason one of the most frequently heard slogans involving divorced persons is "We tried to stay together for the children's sake." Mothers and fathers will often delay a divorce for years out of consideration for the children, even if they are unable substantively to resolve the issues that plague their marriage. Frequently, both fathers and mothers put forth heroic efforts to make things all right for the children, no matter what the circumstances of the actual divorce. When these efforts result in a more positive life for one's children, divorce can seem a healthy decision instead of a failure. As a divorced father said in a *USA Today* article on divorce, "One good parent has to be better than two who fight all the time."[6]

Parents who remain with their children after a divorce discover a special connectedness with them, just as parents who are separated from their sons or daughters after divorce experience deep loneliness and pain. This special connectedness that divorced parents feel between themselves and their children is a lifeline to meaning. It is as if one's child is a link with one's deepest memories. If divorce is an unexpected fork in the road, it is also a leaving of the path that one hoped for. One strikes off in a new direction that is far less secure and far lonelier than one could foresee, even if it is clear that the divorce was necessary. As a divorced person begins this lonely

[21]

pilgrimage on the unanticipated path, one's son or daughter suddenly becomes a special companion who reminds one of the meaning of life and who offers an antidote to one's sense of loss and disappointment. Children anchor one's memories so that life does not drift off into despair. Their presence leads one to recall the most beguiling family moments: the stories that we read to our son before a fire or the pride we saw on our daughter's face when she performed a difficult pirouette on ice. The early stages of divorce tempt us to laugh bitterly at the illusion of love, to say cynically that giving one's self to another is a naive act that foolishly opens one to hurt. When we are blinded by such bitter musings, the companionship of our child becomes a flower that blooms in the middle of the coldest winter. Conversely, when that child is missing, life seems like a winter cornfield in Wisconsin that is filled with nothing but barren stalks. A student wrote:

> When my daughter went with her father on Saturdays, I thought I was going to die! It made me think of the future and how alone I would be when all my children were gone. The prospect of being alone with myself, a person I didn't love, for the rest of my life was pretty frightening.

Such feelings are natural. We should recognize them and work through them so that we do not need our children to protect us from the pain involved in divorce. If we are not able to admit that we are depending heavily on our children's presence to cope with our own grief, we will discover that we are inadvertently involved in controversy with our ex-spouse and are not healing from our divorce.

It is important to recognize that the very fact that divorcing parents love their children so desperately and wish to protect them from the pain of divorce so intensely may lead the parents into a situation in which they are contesting each other for custody of their children. Custody battles do not always grow out of a concern for what is best for the children. More frequently than we like to admit, custody issues also involve our need to demonstrate that we are good parents and that we are valued by our children. I am not suggesting that parents are always selfish or petty about this issue. Rather, I want to point out that in the early stages of divorce, husbands and wives have a complex relationship with their children that can involve both nurture and dependency. In our strongest moments of parenting, we guide, nourish, and support our offspring. But when we feel weak we may turn to them in the hope that they will feed us with their love.

Divorce is such a weak moment. Many times we may want very badly to empower our children, but our emotional pain makes it difficult to give. We may feel unworthy or "defective" after our divorce and reach out for our children to assure us that we are valuable people. It is so easy to encourage our children to fill this role. Indeed, children virtually leap into the void to heal the pain of a parent who is struggling through depression. All else has been ripped from our grasp. Why should we not enjoy the embrace and encouragement of our children during this difficult time? And why should we not pour out even more extravagant love on them, since they are undoubtedly traumatized by the loss of a mother or father? They deserve additional affection and so do we. What could be needed more? Nothing is wrong with an honest affection between divorced people and their children. Indeed, caring communication and a mutual opening of our lives is a major factor in healing from emotional injuries. Divorced parents and their children need to practice this kind of intimacy with each other in order to make their peace with pain and loss and move on to a new stage of life. What is critical to be aware of is that intimate sharing between divorcing parent and child needs to occur freely and not compulsively.

Free intimacy is expressed in the natural inclination of people who love one another to hear, know, and support. It is reflected in the desire of people who suffer to be seen and understood. This mode of free intimacy is one that does not seek dependency relationships in order to buttress the crumbling walls of one's life. Rather, it is a communion based on the conviction that deep sharing between people is healing.

By contrast, compulsive intimacy between a divorcing parent and child is characterized by the use of a son's or daughter's love as a coping mechanism for the parent's own loneliness and as a means for "proving" that he or she is still worthwhile. As long as this style of using one's child to document the value of one's life occurs, the pain of divorce will continue. This is the case because compulsive intimacy keeps one from confronting the heart of their pain.

It is important for divorced people to ponder this paradox of intimacy with their children. On the one hand, divorce may bring a parent and child closer than ever before. Deeper sharing may occur. The health of the children may improve. Such signs are indications that a divorce was a positive decision. They help to redeem a broken relationship. They also offer those who divorce one of the few areas in which they can feel pride in a divorce because the separation has resulted in a situation in which their children are growing in positive ways. On the other hand, as we have seen, an unhealthy dependency relationship can also occur between divorced parents and their children, which undermines the healing process. Only by being sensitive to both dimensions of this paradox can an empowering relationship occur.

Of course, children are not only a link between divorced parents and their fondest memories. When they suffer because of divorce, sons and daughters multiply their parents' sense of guilt, grief, and pain. Even when their emotional hardship has no relationship with the divorce, parents are tempted to feel that the breakup of their marriage is somehow to blame. One woman told a tale of tragedy in the lives of her children after she divorced. Her story aches with the respon-

[24]

sibility she felt for their fate. It bears witness to the enormous effort divorced women and men must put forth in order to overcome feelings of failure.

When divorce finally came I recall a tremendous sense of relief and a feeling of freedom. The rebirthing process had been slow and very painful but also very steady and filled with joy. Since I was sexually abused within marriage and a virgin at the time of marriage, my recovery into joy was and is a sometimes-frantic cacophony. A healing relationship has been central in that recovery. Resolving how the children have been affected has been much more difficult. The oldest sons—then eleven and thirteen—were in the custody of their father. My nine-year-old daughter and four-year-old son were in my custody. The oldest son became the brunt of my ex-husband's rage and suffered abuse from the age of thirteen until his father kicked him out of the house on his eighteenth birthday. The second son was killed in an automobile accident at the age of sixteen, and my daughter became pregnant at the age of fifteen. The youngest son will be fourteen in December and seems the least damaged by the divorce experience. By the grace of God, our oldest son and only daughter are currently in private, church-related colleges, and I expect their healing to continue. After nearly ten years I am finally able to believe that God forgives me and loves me still. The failure I felt for not being able to make my marriage work and not being able to accept God's forgiveness—not even being able to forgive myself—left me with deep, deep, anger for a long, long time.

This poignant story reminds us how frequently divorce is accompanied by feelings of uncleanness. When our children suffer after our divorce, our immediate emotional reaction is to feel responsible. It is as if divorce is a contagious pain that infects and soils the lives of all who are touched by it. If we had not decided to divorce, we feel, our children would not be suffering. If it were not for the fact that we were failures as parents, our children would not be burdened by heartache

[25]

and pain. These voices cause us to feel yet another pang of guilt about our divorce. Again and again I received statements from people that read like the following: "When I got divorced I felt like a failure, unlovable, ugly, that I had no desirable qualities. I thought my family was broken up and that I had broken it up. I thought I should have been better; that there were answers I should have known and things I should have done." Yet the pain that our children feel in the middle of our divorce sometimes gives us the chance to meet them on that rare ground of human suffering where some of the deepest human relationships occur.

When our children suffer because their family unit breaks, we are reminded that parenting is not just inspiring, nurturing, and empowering. It is also teaching our children how to cope with the partiality of life and relationships. Parenthood, therefore, involves the need for mothers and fathers explicitly to confess the limits of their own emotional strength so that their children can learn how to deal with their own weaknesses and painful experiences of loss as they are confronted with them.

As we delve into the experiences of family life, we are discovering that interludes of deep sharing can occur between children and parents during moments of brokenness. Once we believed that the family's role was to be a citadel of stability. Parents were to bear up under every adversity and triumph over every tribulation, including divorce or the death of a spouse. However, as we have come to see that such an image has little of reality in it, we have been surprised also to discover that parents have received nurture, friendship, and support from their children precisely when they have been devastated by loss and grief, feel inadequate, and no longer perceive themselves to be in a meaningful guardian role over their children. At such times divorced parents discover that they no longer have to protect their children from the difficult realities of divorce by being strong for them, but instead can share their pain and mourn honestly with them. It's OK for parents and children to go through rocky times together after a divorce. We should expect the divorced to experience moments of disorientation, grief, and disillusionment before a new equilibrium occurs. We should anticipate that children will feel "distant" from their mothers and fathers after a divorce and that parents will feel "weak" and indecisive in front of their children. We should expect moments of emotional sniping and temperamental volatility that result from having one's physical space and traditions uprooted by circumstances beyond one's control. Divorced families, to say nothing of the culture at large, need to accept the fact that the emotions experienced cannot be patched up overnight and that the people involved cannot simply be stoic in the middle of a series of events that takes years to resolve. Then, perhaps, we should be prepared to offer the kind of support that is most needed: sharing our woundedness with one another and patiently seeking for healing possibilities together. Although it is important for divorcing parents to develop the capacity to share their feelings with their children, this is an emotional evolution that has yet to occur. A landmark study known as the California Children of Divorce Project tracked 131 children from divorced families for five years. Judith Wallerstein and Joan Kelley, the two architects of the study, discovered that 80 percent of the youngest children were *unaware* that their parents were going to divorce and coped with the situation in a willy-nilly fashion after the actual separation. In an unrelated study, author Warner Troy found the same dynamic to be occurring within the families he contacted.

The statistics suggest plainly that one parent usually is left with the burden of explaining the divorce and helping the children to heal from the pain. Characteristically, this burden falls on the mother. Husbands often tend to leave without having spent any time with their sons or daughters. As one woman wrote:

[27]

I was so traumatized and dazed by my husband's decision to simply walk out on twenty years of marriage with twenty minutes of one-way dialogue that it was several months before I even began to accept that his decision was anything except the result of a mental breakdown or midlife crisis. He spoke not one word to his young adult children, leaving them in agony and confusion.

Another woman explained the frustration she felt in being left with the responsibility for both fighting for financial support from her ex-husband and somehow explaining the situation to her children:

What the court can't write into your decree is human parental responsibility. It can't keep a man from being intentionally fired from his well-paying job to go on unemployment so he won't have to support his children, while he lives with and is supported by another woman. When you scream, "Contempt of the court order!" it can't keep him from suddenly leaving the state without a word while your eight-year-old son cries for his father and accuses you of being the reason he is gone.

My ex-husband has returned to the state and the children see him occasionally, speak to him by phone occasionally. Regardless of my prior frustration with him, he is still their biological father, and at their young age they love him unconditionally, which is something I have to work through and accept for their sakes. I can now speak to him without my stomach churning, and although he owes me literally thousands in back support payments, I know in my heart I will never take him to court again for it. Given the type of person he is, a runner, it would not be worth the pain and suffering it causes everyone, especially the children.

There are several reasons why parents do not share their decision to divorce with their children. In most cases the silence grows out of protective concern. Parents do not want to burden their children with their own problems and often feel unable to confide awkward situations, such as sexual problems or abusive situations. One divorced man wrote that he felt great relief in dealing with a sexual stalemate that had made his marriage unworkable. He said, *"Finally, I would deal with myself and with the issues long suppressed."* But he also noted how stressful it was to share the reasons for his divorce with his children:

> I couldn't comprehend co-parenting two college-aged daughters. I had identified myself for the previous ten years as "bisexual" but knew I was really homosexually oriented. How to accept this, live with it, and share it with the significant people in my life, including my daughters, was difficult.

On the one hand, it is easy to avoid such difficult sharing with the assumption that our children are not "ready" to peer beneath the surface of our parental veneer. Perhaps they will no longer respect or love us. Perhaps the realities they discover will be untenable for them, and they will draw away from us. On the other hand, we may feel that our sharing of a pending divorce with our children will pressure them to take sides. We may say nothing to them about the circumstances of the divorce so as not to put them in the position of deciding who is to blame for killing their family. Fundamentally, we avoid confiding in our children about divorce because we feel so damned guilty about what we are doing to them in order to save the integrity of our own lives. A woman wrote:

> Guilt is one of the hardest emotions to deal with. The guilt about the marriage is mostly over. To some extent, being able to blame the other person in both rational and irrational ways helped with that. The hardest guilt to deal with is the guilt over breaking up my children's family and that somehow in the process of that I have made everything more difficult for them. The feeling that instead of helping your children you have contributed to hurting them is very difficult to deal with. In

my case, all of the children have some rather pronounced problems stemming from either the divorce or the way the relationship existed in the marriage.

While I am at the point that I can't think of one reason that I would want to be married to my ex-husband, I still have problems in trying to disentangle myself with relationships with him because of the children. I think that the image I can't give up is that of a mother and father who can work together for the good of the children.

Sharing such feelings with one's children seems important. There are at least two essential reasons why this should be so. First, as we have seen, the sharing of our woundedness in divorce is a mode of confession, a way of telling our children what is real in our lives. Second, the sharing of our feelings about divorce is a teaching mechanism that helps our children to understand the complex texture of life: how it feels to be emotionally injured; how it feels to be betrayed; how it feels to have dreams smashed; how it feels to be powerless to heal relationships. We too often assume that mothers and fathers best benefit their children by giving advice. But advice is cheap. When we give it we do not customarily share our life experiences with our offspring. Instead, we offer "shoulds," "oughts," truisms, and platitudes that do little to sharpen their perceptions about the ambiguous nature of life.

One of the fundamental reasons why sharing the reality of divorce with our children is so meaningful is that such confiding has impact. It is a sharing that cannot be ignored. It is the kind of unpretentious meeting that horizontalizes the relationship between parent and child, no matter the ages of those who are involved. At such times a new dimension of knowing one another emerges. Parents find themselves teaching through the pain in their lives, and children understand what it means to respond with compassion to grief that cannot be erased.

Divorce has the potential of teaching that all of us confront huge hurdles of hurt in our lives and that all of us need to share that hurt if we hope to heal. In a paradoxical way it may be that divorced people whose children are alienated from them because of the separation have the opportunity to share in the deepest way: by confessing their own pain, by exploring opportunities for mutual healing of grief, and by envisioning a new family constellation that is vital and hopeful.

The possibility of healing with pain has been convincingly presented in such works as *Compassion,* by Matthew Fox, and *The Wounded Healer,* by Henri Nouwen. The historical church has made great strides since the 1970s in setting before the culture the fact that those who grieve have a right to their pain and that people around them have a responsibility to honor that right rather than try to explain it away. Despite our culture's tendency to avoid pain, we also are more aware than any generation in recent memory of the need to name the *reality* of painful life experiences and surrender to such experiences honestly rather than deny them. A divorced woman noted how familiar we have become with the grief stages involved in divorce:

> It seems almost redundant these days to list the stages that people go through during initial separation—many trade books discuss them well. The stages differ in length and intensity and in the sequence they follow. For me they were shock, grief, anger, panic, elation, loneliness, acceptance, and personal growth. . . . Almost all divorcing people are obsessed with trying to understand what went wrong. Each person must work this out for herself or himself.

The need to understand what went wrong is a concern around which divorced people do much sharing. Such sharing might be with a therapeutic source, such as a counselor or a pastor. But it might also be with friends who are present with us in our pain and offer understanding. One divorced man described his supportive friendships in the following way:

> My friends were people who could supply physical closeness
> . . . hugs and hand-holding without any sexual overtones. The
> freedom for the physical expression of feelings and the need for
> closeness was very important for me.

To be understood, touched, and affirmed is essential when
one is healing from divorce. Such support gives one a sense of
hope when the evidence of one's life suggests that meaning is
hopelessly broken. Friends give us the courage and strength
to fly again. They encourage us to trust that part of us which
knows that our divorce is a tragic, but necessary, decision.

Friends help us to discover that divorce, even though it is a
death, is also a flight of freedom. There is almost always a
sense of liberation that accompanies the end of a marriage.
Thus virtually all the stories of divorced men and women state
that feelings of failure, fear, anger, and depression are counterpointed by a paradoxical enthusiasm about beginning
again. Seemingly, these feelings of freedom result from the
fact that most people feel that they have been in an unhealthy
relationship for far too long. Divorce, then, is often a reassert-
ing of control over a life that has literally stalemated. This is
particularly true in the case of a couple who has lived for many
years in conditions of estrangement. When divorce comes it is
a relief, a breath of fresh air. A couple who responded jointly
to my questionnaire explained the feelings of relief that accompanied their divorce—after sixteen years of marriage—in
the following way. The husband wrote: "My main feeling during the divorce was one of guilt, that I probably should have
tried longer and harder to 'make it work.' But the truth is that
I had actually tried too hard and too long. Both of my sons told
me that." In a similar vein the wife wrote: "My feelings and
mental anguish were of a six-year period before the actual
divorce. Once my husband and I parted the turmoil was about
over. We parted as friends."

This experience of relief is common. The results of a Uni-
versity of Colorado study, which interviewed 153 women and

men, suggest that the highest incidence of stress symptoms involved in divorce occur, not after divorce, but six months before. It is as if the separating moment is a release from the prison of an angry, alienated marriage. Several people who were questioned shared their feelings of relief that accompanied divorce:

I began to look at the positive side: I didn't have to tolerate his anger. He was always angry—I never knew about what—but he was always angry.

*   *   *

Relief was the first, and at times overwhelming, emotion.

*   *   *

The first emotion felt at the moment of separation was relief: the pressure is off! This is the first day of the rest of my life! This emotion was short-lived, as it was soon replaced by fear that I wouldn't make it, wouldn't handle all the responsibilities that I now must assume alone.

*   *   *

After the separation my ex-husband repeatedly said that he didn't want a divorce. I was certain that I did. I experienced a mix of feeling—guilt because he said I was killing him, anger because of the manipulation, and a new sense of freedom, courage, and joy because I was finally making decisions for myself and learning to like myself.

*   *   *

My feelings and emotions were centered mostly on if I could make it on my own with three young children. Also, I wondered if I was denying my children what other families had: the security of a father and mother, both in the same home. But I also felt that I could not keep up the pretense of being happy in a home where I was being physically and mentally abused. My children (especially the oldest one) saw this happen at different times and I felt it couldn't continue. It took me

[33]

over six months to accept the fact that it was for the best that we were going through this divorce and another six months to see that it was best for my children, because they were more relaxed, or maybe I should say relieved, and I found that things were not as bad as I imagined, on my own.

The time before divorce is a soul-grinding state. As one analyst describes it, it is the time when we come to recognize that our marriage cannot be healed. We see the depth of woundedness that litters the home and wonder for the first time, "How much more pain can I take?" During this period, suppressed resentments may erupt and grievances may be aired. When the separation finally occurs it is an anticlimax, a calm after the battle. This coexistence of regret and expectation adds greatly to the emotional complexity of divorce, and that complexity can confuse those who are divorcing. These feelings tempt us to believe that we can finally pursue dreams that have been deadlocked for years. Yet the optimism is tentative. We are not sure that we deserve such freedom. We are not sure whether we are a "liberated" person or a "failure," and in this bold contradiction lies much of the difficulty of healing from divorce.

The key to healing is to surrender to both sides of the contradiction. One must taste both freedom and regret before one can journey through the grief of divorce. If, on the one hand, one focuses only on self-condemnation, one ignores the redemptive possibilities that occur in the middle of broken marriages and one may stifle opportunities to begin again despite life's tragedy and one's own mistakes. If, on the other hand, one focuses only on the fantasy that divorce is a flight of freedom, one overlooks one's complicity in a marriage that did not work and one may lose the opportunity to discover one's own nature on a more profound level.

Divorce ultimately demands humility. It forces us to acknowledge that no human being is guaranteed faithful relationships. Divorce teaches us that when we find ourselves in intimate relationship, it is far more of a gift than an achievement. Divorce is the recognition of the limits of our own capacity to "make" relationships "work." In our moments of connectedness we build fanciful notions of our power and authority. We pretend that we can finesse relationships, cultivate affection, and manufacture love by doing the right things. When, despite our best intentions and efforts, our marriage slips from our grasp, we discover the illusion of such thinking and are led to accept the limits of our power. Authentic expectancy after a divorce is a sensitivity that must be earned. We earn it, not by triumphing over the loss of a love, but by persevering through our exile from a home that we have loved. I like Alice Walker's insight:

> I awoke to the bitter knowledge that in order just to continue to love the land of my birth, I was expected to leave it. For black people—including my parents—had learned a long time ago that to stay willingly in a beloved but brutal place is to risk losing the love and being forced to recognize only the brutality.[7]

So it is with divorce. In an estranged marriage we come to see that love is gradually being lost and that little remains but a brutal emptiness. Loneliness echoes like ghost voices in a house once filled with laughter, and we are forced to accept the fact that to stay is not to risk the possibility of reconciliation, but of the further loss of love. It is to choose macabre estrangement, which is far more brutal than the decision to leave one's home. And so one says good-bye. The flight of freedom, bittersweet as it is, has begun. There is no bon voyage celebration, no sense of quest; one is simply grateful that the decision finally has been made. One is terrified that there will be a crash landing, yet one limps along on weak, erratic wings, pursuing a tenuous future and hoping somehow to find a place of rest and peace.

[35]

CHAPTER TWO

Of Judgment and Grace

Historically, the church has had great difficulty in arriving at a mature and balanced view of marriage and divorce. Through the early centuries, marriage was perceived as an encumbrance to those who were waiting for the second coming of Christ and, later, preparing for martyrdom. Paul counseled the church at Corinth that history was in its final stages and Christians should refrain from marrying unless it was impossible for them to control their sexual desire (1 Corinthians 7:8–9). He further observed that unmarried Christians have fewer distractions and therefore more opportunities to "please the Lord" (1 Corinthians 7:32–35).

The Church Fathers also issued warnings against the married life. Ambrose, for instance, suggested that marriage was a sensual "slumber" that distracted people from the reality of God:

> What is that sleep for a short period of time except the fact that when we turn our soul to be united with someone in marriage, we seem to lower and close eyes that were intent on the Kingdom of God for a kind of slumber here in the world and are asleep to divine things for a while as we rest in the fleeting affairs of earth.[1]

Tertullian, although married, also believed that matrimony was a distraction to the Christian life. He argued that virginity and continence were superior to an involved marriage and wrote, in a private correspondence to his wife:

Why are we anxious to have children when we want to leave them once we have them for fear of the impending trials? Are we not eager ourselves to be quit of this sinful age and received into the presence of the Lord as even the Apostles desired? Offspring are hardly needful to the servant of God. . . . Why did the Lord prophesy, "Woe to the pregnant and nursing," except to bear witness that this baggage of family cares will be an encumbrance on that day of departure that is to come?[2]

An unknown bishop in the early church formally urged Christians to avoid sex and childbirth:

Let us be mindful of others too and abstain from having many children. Let us give more of ourselves to prayer and the service of God, looking forward to the day of judgement. Thus we for our part will not be weighed down by the baggage of earthly concerns, and they will not be faced with something that we ourselves are afraid of.[3]

In the late fourth century such proclamations became even more strident. Jerome wrote:

Woe to the women that are with child or nursing these days. The forest grows thick to be cut down someday later. The field is sown to be harvested. The world is already full. The land does not hold us up. . . . It is not harlots who are threatened here with doom, not houses of prostitution, which no one doubts will be condemned, but swelling wombs and crying babies and the fruits and works of marriage.[4]

Augustine went so far as to suggest that those who did not marry were hastening the kingdom:

I know some will complain: "What if all men wished to abstain from sexual relations? How would the human race survive?" If only all men would have such a wish! . . . The City of God would be filled much more quickly and the end of the world made to come sooner. What else does the Apostle seem to urge when he says on this point, "I would wish that all were like myself," or in that passage, "I say this however, brethren: the

[37]

time is short. It remains that those who have wives be as though they did not have them"? From all this it seems to me that in this present age only those who lack self-control should marry.[5]

It might be suggested that for the first three centuries of the church's life, marriage was aggressively discouraged and implicit divorce affirmed. In the words of Augustine, the most influential theologian of the early church, "those who have wives [are to] be as though they did not have them." A kind of caste system gradually evolved that glorified celibacy and virginity, celebrated continence in marriage, and tolerated what we today conceive of as a whole and healthy relationship. In the face of Protestant assertions that virginity or celibacy was not essential for the living of a faithful Christian life, the sixteenth-century Council of Trent made a definitive theological statement:

> If anyone says that the married state is of a higher rank than the state of virginity or celibacy and that it is not better and more blessed to remain in virginity or celibacy than to be joined in matrimony, let him be anathema.[6]

Thus early Christians were taught to perceive marriage as a second-class life-style and divorce, whether implicitly or explicitly, as a legitimate option for faith formation. The early church permitted divorce if one wished to enter the priesthood and also advocated disciplines of abstinence through which couples were to pretend that they were not married. So popular was this discipline that a formal disposition was created that required bishops and presbyters to live separately from their wives.[7]

Robert Rainey offers a compelling synopsis of the early church's view of marriage:

> The practice of self-denial for its own sake was regarded and commended as an eminent Christian virtue. As embraced by

Christians it applied to food and raiment, but it had a very special application to marriage. . . . The Christians, on the whole, maintained the legitimacy of marriage as a divine institution, and an appointed part of the order of the world; but it was habitual for those who led sentiment on this point to think and speak of a concession to the weaknesses of human nature, and as a fixing of life on a level lower than the highest. Hence, though marriage was always guarded against the imputation of being in itself evil, yet entrance into married life could hardly be disassociated, as it seemed, from a certain sense of inferiority, and abstinence implied a superior virtue. Early in the second century, Christians who have renounced marriage and been faithful to this purpose during their lives are spoken of and pointed to with satisfaction.[8]

It would be a mistake to believe that all early Christians felt this way. As early as the third century, such thinkers as Clement of Alexandria challenged the assumption that marriage had to be seen as an inferior alternative to a life of celibacy or continence. Rather, they suggested that marriage was a spiritual gift to which some Christians were called by God. In this respect Clement said: "He eats and drinks and takes a wife, not for their own sake and as his chief concern, but led by necessity. And when I say 'takes a wife,' I mean if the Word has said to."[9] Fulgentius of Ruspe was another who perceived that marriage was a spiritual gift:

The Lord himself has bound them together with the bond of fidelity, favored them with the gift of his blessing, multiplied them by the addition of children. . . . For we confess that the fidelity of marriage is from God. . . . "Each has his own gift from God, etc." We too recognize the distinctive rank of each gift and do not deny that each has been given to the faithful by God.[10]

By around A.D. 1000 this remnant strain within the church became a significant voice. Increasing numbers of theologians began to suggest that marriage was a religious order, ordained by God. German preacher Berthold of Ratisbonne spoke stridently for this new understanding:

> God has sanctified marriage more than any other order in the world, more than the discalced friars, the friar's preacher, or the gray monks. In one point they cannot be compared with holy marriage: we cannot do without that order. Therefore, God has commanded it. The others he has only recommended. . . . How would heaven be filled without marriage?[11]

The church gradually inverted its early understanding of marriage. As marriage once was seen as a distraction to the Christian life, it now was perceived as the most sanctified religious order in the world. Where once abstinence in marriage was seen as the way to populate the City of God, now fruitfulness in marriage is perceived as the way to fill heaven.

Jesuit scholar Joseph Kerns, on whose research much of this chapter depends, suggests that the definitive shift in the church's theology of marriage came in the sixteenth century. He cites the catalyst for this shift as the influential work *Third ABC of the Spiritual Life* by De Ossuna:

> In his *Third ABC of the Spiritual Life*, so prized by saints and mystics during the 1500's, De Ossuna declares that married people belong to an order, not of Dominic or Francis, or Peter, but of one founded by the Father in Eden, approved by the Son at Cana, and confirmed by the Holy Spirit, who gives the couple his grace on wedding day. From this time on theologians kept repeating that marriage is as truly a gift of God as consecrated virginity.[12]

Once the church agreed that marriage was as genuine a gift as celibacy or virginity, it began conceptually to ennoble God's place in marriage. Theologians went to great lengths to proclaim that God ordained every marriage and worked a divine will in every relationship, regardless of its quality. De la Puente, for instance, speculated that prayerful Christians would find the appropriate mate with the aid of guardian angels:

> From all this we gather that one who desires to make a good election in the matter should with prayer and confidence have recourse to the guardian angels. They are the invisible match-makers and instruments for directing marriages and leading them to a happy ending.[13]

As the church came more and more to celebrate marriage as a state of grace, it also became increasingly intolerant of divorce. Once estrangement and annulment were used in the early centuries to rid oneself of distractions that kept one from union with God. However, if God empowers every marriage, then divorce, far from being a road to a deeper religious life, is tantamount to a rebellion against God's sovereignty in the matter of matrimony. Thus we find theologians such as Francis de Sales insisting that all marriages should endure in the knowledge that God will redeem even the most estranged relationships:

> There are others who have not been called at all. Nevertheless, since they have come, their vocation has been made good and ratified by God. . . . His liberality is so great that He gives these means to those to whom he has not promised them and has not obliged Himself since he did not call them.[14]

In a much plainer manner of speaking, the French priest Masillon said:

> It is clear that the Lord has in no way at all resided in your choice if imprudence, human respect, and passions alone have formed a state in life for you; your life is to be pitied, I admit, but not despaired of. . . . To the grief of an improper choice, God can accord the graces He would not have accorded to a legitimate choice. Outwardly, you are not in His scheme of things, but your heart always is when it is giving itself to Him.[15]

[41]

Once again, I want to refer to Joseph Kerns, who succinctly summarizes these theological perspectives:

> Even ill-sorted husbands and wives cannot therefore conclude that God has not given them to each other. Whether their marriage is their own fault or came about through some mistake for which they could not really be blamed, if it was valid, it was a gift from God.[16]

The Protestant Reformation did not particularly clarify the confusion over marriage and divorce. Although it legitimated marriage by allowing clergy to marry, the Reformers themselves expressed great ambivalence about the married state. Martin Luther was particularly inconsistent in this respect. While he spoke with romantic and bawdy intensity about the consolations of the married state, he also perceived sexuality as a remnant of the fall. Of his own sexual relations he said, "This cools my blood," yet he also suggested marriage was an "emergency hospital for the illness of human drives."[17]

In the same way, John Calvin perceived marriage as companionship. Yet, as James Nelson has pointed out, Calvin felt that Christian couples needed to legislate their sexual relations—not enjoying them too much, but keeping them within the temperate realm of "delicacy and propriety."[18] This ambiguous appreciation of marriage was counterpointed by an equally ambiguous understanding of divorce. Luther, for instance, was opposed to divorce. Yet, on occasion, he suggested that bigamy was an acceptable alternative (for men), arguing that multiple marriages had been enjoyed by the Old Testament patriarchs with divine approval and was never explicitly condemned in the New Testament.[19]

The Reformed churches and the Anabaptists allowed divorce from the beginning—primarily for reasons of maintaining a cohesive community of faith. The Anabaptists, whose discipline it was to live out a New Testament life based on the teachings of the Sermon on the Mount, tolerated no mixed marriages. If only one spouse joined the Anabaptist community, his or her marriage was declared dissolved. For Calvinists, marriages were to be terminated if one spouse refused to follow the other into exile for the sake of the gospel.[20] As Christian faith began to spread in America, yet another perspective developed. The "Protestant temperament," as Philip Greven calls it, gave rise to a dutiful view of marriage, just as it gave rise to a dutiful view of life. Marriage was not to be entered into for reasons of love, fulfillment, companionship, or sexual gratification. Rather, the decision to marry was to be a response to the will of God, as ratified by one's parents. In this early American context a Christian was raised with the expectation that his or her emotions should be rigorously controlled and self-disciplined so that one could live a virtuous life, pleasing to God. This attitude can plainly be identified in the following tale of a twenty-eight-year-old Quaker named David Ferris:

> After residing in Philadelphia about six months, and having joined the Society of Friends, he "began to think of settling" himself, "and to marry, when the way would appear without obstruction. . . ." He decided that marriage "was honorable to all who married from pure motives, to the right person, and in the proper time and way, as divine Providence should direct." He was convinced that it was "essential that all men should seek for wisdom, and wait for it, to guide them in this important undertaking; because no man, without divine assistance, is able to discover who is the right person for him to marry; but the Creator of both can and will direct him."[21]

Ferris encountered a young woman who attracted him, and he went to visit her and her mother. He had not been there but a half hour when he heard "something like a still small voice, saying to me, 'Seekest thou great things for thyself?—seek not.' This language pierced me like a sword to the heart."[22] Ferris left quickly and felt "confused and benumbed." He feared that he would never be permitted to marry. In time he met another woman while dining at a friend's house but "took very little notice of her [until] a language very quietly, very pleasantly, passed through my mind, on this wise, 'If thou wilt marry that young woman, thou shalt be happy with her.' "[23]

For weeks Ferris resisted marriage, discovering, at last, that "it pleased the Lord, once, more clearly to show me that if I would submit, it should not only tend to my happiness, but that a blessing should rest on my posterity."[24] "Fully resigned," he then waited another six months to receive his parents' consent.

In this context, marriage is not so much a romantic involvement between two persons who seek to lose themselves in committed relationship as it is a relationship arranged by God and consented to by parents. In some cases this view may have honored the emotional needs of young women and men, but in many other cases it pressured them to "submit" to marriages deemed suitable by their parents or suggested to them by the hyperactive superegos that were so much a part of the Protestant temperament. The correspondence of a young, eighteenth-century Puritan man points out how radically young people deferred to their parents in the matter of marriage:

> I am very glad I think so much like my Honoured Parents with respect to marriage. I shall never think I am at liberty to dispose of myself without their consent who gave me being, and if I should ever be so mad as to do it, tho you shoud forgive me, I shoud never forgive myself.[25]

Compulsive submission in the matter of marriage was most radically visited on women. Shulamith Firestone has noted that wives were forced by law to defer to their husbands through the nineteenth century. She asserts that the early American women's rights movement was based on the fact

[44]

that women had no civil status under the law, including the fact that they were pronounced civilly dead after marriage and could not have custody of their children if they divorced.[26]

In the eighteenth and nineteenth centuries, then, divorce was a rare option. On the one hand, marriages in the Puritan context were a matter of submitting to God's plan and the blessings given by one's parents. To break such an arrangement was unimaginable. If one had ill feelings about one's marriage, one must recognize that the difficulty lay not in the marriage, but in the sins and corruptions of one's heart. This was particularly true of the zealous evangelicals. As Phillip Greven puts it:

> By controlling their own behavior rigorously, evangelicals sought to suppress their unacceptable feelings and thoughts. Any deviation, any omission might threaten them with the emergence of inadmissible feelings and desires. They could not tolerate much personal freedom or flexibility. There was too much danger in not adhering to the rules that governed their lives. . . . They found reassurance in following the Will of God, knowing that their own wills had been conquered and had been surrendered altogether.[27]

Even as this mind-set softened to allow for independent thought and the possibility of self-gratification, women continued to be functionally precluded from exercising the option of divorce. As we have seen, the cost of divorce was so high that few women dared to separate from their husbands, no matter the quality of the marriage. In such a cultural context, the church quite naturally became accustomed to inveighing against divorce while losing its capacity to respond compassionately to those whose marriages had died. There was, after all, little call for a ministry to divorced Christians through the first 150 years of American culture. In the twentieth century the situation changed dramatically. Today nearly half the marriages end in divorce. No longer is marriage a sacred obligation to which one must submit, but a relationship through

[45]

which men and women seek fulfillment. As Max Lerner observes in *America as a Civilization:*

> American marriage has developed a new area of vulnerability. With the quest for happiness, as with the fight for social equality, great expectations feed on themselves, and every new gain means a more critical view of the gap that remains between reality and promise. The high divorce rate does not necessarily mean that there is more unhappiness than there was in American marriages, but only that there is less propensity to accept unhappiness as part of the eternal frame of things that cannot be mended.[28]

In the middle of this radical cultural change, the church is divided. Some interpreters, such as Pope John Paul, call for a return to moral discipline and traditional values, arguing that divorce is a "plague." Other Christians suggest that it is time for the church to learn that there are times when divorce is justified and even healthy. As the first believe that it is critical to proclaim that divorce is a sin, the second suggest that the more essential task is to talk about the meaning of healing in an era in which divorce is nearly a norm, to enter into compassionate dialogue with divorced men and women, and to discover together God's place in the lives of those whose marriages have ended.

We see, then, that the church is not, and never has been, of one mind in its views of marriage and divorce. Rather, the church's teaching and ministry have been contextual. They have, in other words, been shaped largely by the cultural milieu and life experiences of those who interpreted the Christian faith to a particular generation. For this reason we find the widest extremes of proclamation. In the early church, interpreters suggest that marriage is an inferior state and a distraction to the religious life. They further assert that it is appropriate to annul marriages in order to pursue the religious life or to divorce implicitly by behaving as if one had no

[46]

spouse. In later centuries, theologians image marriage as the greatest of religious orders and speak stridently of the indissolubility of the religious life. During the Reformation, divorce is permitted on a number of grounds, and where it is prohibited, bigamy is suggested as a faithful alternative by Luther.

The church needs to make up its ecclesiastical mind about several essential issues related to divorce. Is marriage inherently indissoluble, or are there times when vows end? Is divorce inevitably a sin, or are there sometimes good reasons, which God blesses, for ending a marriage? How does God feel when a marriage is possessed by an agony of estrangement? Finally, how is the church to minister with divorced Christians in the name of Christ?

Several recent interpreters have suggested that these questions need to be addressed in a manner that holds in tension the doctrine of the sanctity of marriage on the one hand and support for the divorced on the other. For instance, in her article "Clergy, Divorce, and Remarriage," Sandra Brown suggests that the frequency of divorce has forced the church to restore the balance between two seemingly contradictory elements of doctrine: the proclamation that God's will is permanence in marriage and the proclamation that God forgives those who fail to live up to this ideal. Brown suggests that it is the church's task to offer a theology and a ministry to the divorced that combines "truth" and "grace," "confronting" and "comforting," with firm insistence on a threefold healing ministry that involves confession, repentance, and forgiveness.[29]

A renewed ministry to divorced Christians needs more compassion and less judgment. If we the church want to combine confronting and comforting in a new way, we must begin by withholding moralistic proclamations about divorce and listening to the actual experiences of divorcing Christians. When one begins to listen in this way, one discovers that

[47]

divorced Christians are, in the main, already participating in confession and repentance. What is lacking is encouragement to resolve the heavy feelings of failure and guilt that already burden them. The following stories point this out in striking terms:

> During my marriage I would frequently weep in church because of my sins of omission. In order to keep my family together, to stay married, there were so many things I had to give up that I felt I was not the person God meant me to be.

> *   *   *

> I found myself at many times crying during parts of the sermon or prayer. Many times I think there were tears of sorrow as well as tears asking forgiveness—tears of repentance.

> *   *   *

> Being a minister, I felt like I had failed in my ministry and my church, myself, and the kids. . . . I felt unclean and shameful that this failure in a loving relationship took place. As a minister, I felt ashamed to go to community gatherings for a long time, and at times I still have problems.

> *   *   *

> To God, husband and wife are as one, so my ex-husband's sin of adultery is also my sin until my ex-husband passes away. Then I shall be free. This bothers me very much.

Divorced people need spiritual direction far more than additional opportunities to confess their sins. The pain of divorce consistently leads Christians into an intense life of prayer. In the face of the death of their marriages these men and women seek rescue, relief, and understanding from God. Yet, precisely at this moment, many feel a great spiritual dryness. Their prayers turn to ashes in their mouths, and God seems far away:

[48]

The biggest disappointment was that I believed if I prayed for God to help me work through this, that we could continue to heal our marriage and build ourselves together, but it seemed that the harder I worked at it, the more I prayed, the worse things got. No healing seemed to take place and so I had to accept the inevitable.

* * *

I totally lost my faith during this period. I was angry, bitter, and felt that God had deserted me. My marriage vows, which I felt were sacred, had been betrayed. I tried Bible reading but ended up thinking that God could not possibly love me, and that God was not there for me. Reading Job took me into further despair. Psalms made me feel hopeless. The Gospels asked me to be forgiving, which I had much trouble doing. The minister preached on love and the sanctity of the family. I could not pray to a God who abandoned me.

* * *

I prayed for almost two years that God should turn my marriage around and that prayer has not been answered. I also remember the slogan, "The family that prays together, stays together." I don't believe that anymore. Our whole life revolved around the church for twenty-five years, and it is very hard for me and the children to be involved in church life. I have lost faith in men who happen to be active in the church and question their motives because my husband lived and breathed church and turned the tables on us in the middle of our life. I do feel that God has made me a stronger person. But I cannot continue to hope that Bob will return because when I hope that way and nothing happens, it hurts too much.

My husband left all his close friends, the church, his family. He acts as if the past never existed. He says he is a new person and that the old one is dead. But his body and the past still haunt me, and it was a good past. I guess that is why I can't close the door on the past. I don't think I will ever completely work my way through this experience. I need answers. My husband says, "You were a wonderful wife and mother," and he gave me a beautiful necklace for twenty-five years of service. But please, dear God, I still need an answer, please.

Such stories help us to understand why a ministry of confession and repentance is not helpful to divorced Christians. Faithful men and women who are struggling through a spiritual desert in which they feel abandoned by God need understanding, not reminders that they are sinful. They need encouragement to pray through the dry times and insights that help them to express their disillusionment and anger at God. Perhaps divorcing Christians need a psalm that can help them through a crisis of belief and prayer. Were I the psalmist, this is the prayer I would write:

PSALM 151
A Lament

Where are you, my God? I have requested a simple thing.
I do not ask you to take away the death of my marriage;
I only want to understand it.

I want an answer to this pain that turns my bones to
    brimstone;
I need help to see through the veil of meaninglessness that
    covers my eyes.
Your silence mocks me. I am, like the psalmist, a
    laughingstock.

I have faithfully worshiped you through many seasons;
My babies I have baptized with your cleansing water,
And my father I have buried in your name.

Yet you withhold a mere conceptual answer that comforts.
Why should I believe in your miracles;
In my time of need they seem as fables to me—wishes as
    empty as the air.

Do you wish me to be spiritually maimed?
Am I to limp upon devotional pathways with tender feet and
a bitter spirit?
Those who no longer believe in your saving love surround
me.
They encourage me to drink the wine of forgetfulness and
surrender to despair.

My hours are filled with a dull groaning in my soul;
And yet I say again, "Save me, O God, and heal me!"

To judge suffering people is trivial; to teach them is profound. One of the most relevant ways to offer a teaching
ministry to the divorced is to help them to recognize the place
of anger in their lives. Matthew and Dennis Linn have noted
that anger is outwardly directed pain, as guilt is inwardly
directed pain. During divorce Christians turn their anger not
only against their former spouses, but also against God. At
first glance, anger toward God would seem to make a divorced Christian an even greater sinner. One should be asking God for forgiveness, not complaining. After all, if one has
failed God's desire for a permanent marriage, what right has
one to be angry if God is absent?

If the church were to offer spiritual direction to the divorced, it might offer them ways to recognize that the experience of a broken marriage can point the way to a deeper faith.
Those who divorce, in other words, have the opportunity to
learn how to accept their pain and anger and use it as a form of
prayer. Abraham Heschel wrote:

> The refusal to accept the harshness of God's ways in the name
> of God's love was an authentic form of prayer. Indeed, the
> ancient prophets of Israel were not in the habit of consenting
> to God's harsh judgement and did not simply nod, saying,
> "Thy will be done." They often challenged God as if to say,
> "Thy will be changed." There are some forms of suffering that a

[51]

man must accept with love and bear in silence; there are other agonies to which he must say no.[30]

In commenting on the ways in which anger at God can lead to a deeper faith, Henri Nouwen says: "[Heschel's] attitude shows how close the Jew, who can protest against God, feels to God. When I can only relate to God in terms of submission, I am much more distant from Him than when I question His decrees."[31]

I am not suggesting that divorce is a righteous act. Rather, I am saying that it has the potential to be a faith-forming event, and the church has the responsibility to catalyze this potential. A timely ministry to the divorced will help them not only to grieve through the failure of their marriage, but also to transcend it by reappropriating their horizon of faith. A woman wrote about the kind of central faith issues with which divorced Christians struggle:

> There was a long stretch of time when faith was very dry and I felt that my whole being was one dry, arid void. . . . Part of the reason for the dryness was a struggle of "Why me?" and then really coming to terms with and accepting that bad things can happen to good people and can happen over and over and over. There was also the difficulty of truly accepting that there were no guaranteed happy endings and that I could struggle through all of this just to find myself facing more struggles. While I had always given lip service to these ideas, there was a part of me that was very vested in the idea that at some time this would all end and the problems would be over. Sometimes I wonder if the belief in heaven and an after life doesn't somehow play into holding on to those ideas. If I believe in a heaven filled with glory, is it unreasonable to believe in that glory before death?

A compassionate ministry to the divorced begins with the providing of spiritual direction that encourages faith questions to emerge. These faith questions seek a way through the desert by waiting for the healing presence of God that reveals itself on the journey. Many persons who responded to the questionnaire shared the answers they received from God. The following accounts are representative:

> I know that I prayed and wrote a lot of poetry. The muse sat on my shoulder and God's Holy Spirit never left me alone, never died for me. I sang my lungs off and entered into the stained glass of a cathedral and somehow my sharp edges were worn off.

* * *

> Faith played a major part in helping me to get back on my feet. My journal—kind of an ongoing prayer—helped me to understand what tensions were at work in me.

The Holy Spirit as the muse on one's shoulder is a fascinating image. In Greek mythology the muse is any of nine goddesses who presided over literature, the arts, and the sciences. In a more general sense the muse was the spirit that inspires artists and poets. In Christian terminology the muse on our shoulders during the time of divorce is the Holy Spirit inviting us to exercise creativity in the midst of death. It is the voice that speaks of resurrection possibilities.

When we respond to the muse on our shoulders with creative expression, we begin to let go of our pain. I am not asserting that divorced Christians can control God's healing presence by being creative. Rather, I am suggesting that creativity opens us to healing by taking us out of ourselves. Our creative expression, whether through prayer, poetry, journal keeping, singing, or personal sharing with a friend, exposes us to life's unexpected stimulations. Through them we slowly discover that we are being healed:

> Faith during this time of divorce was an inward, vital, alive journey. I was open to new information and wrote a paper on

the theology of divorce. It was a real healing exercise. God was alive and God's Spirit visited me in numerous, healing, fragmentary, unambiguous moments.

* * *

Faith in God and prayer were the best support system. And that faith went down all kinds of roads to the point where I doubted I had any left. But God never gave up on me. . . . It was God who finally said to me one day nearly a year ago: "Girl, you've grieved and hurt long enough. Let go and live again." I remember that so clearly. I had never before felt my God and my faith so deeply, and a giant weight was lifted. I knew that day that the experience was behind me and I had survived.

* * *

My faith played a major role in my divorce. I refer to some of these months as God's carrying me on eagle's wings. I felt the presence of God's grace in people around me and the tender care of God's spirit during some very long and tearful nights. Through the experience I found renewed courage. My foundations had been shaken and in many ways I felt vulnerable to my core. But at no time did I feel that God was absent. In fact, it was my relationship with God that always carried me through. I kept a journal of prayer and reflections through my divorce and for three years after. To see my own growth through the reflections was very helpful.

* * *

Forgiveness of sins and a fresh start encouraged me especially in my most guilty moments. God's abiding love comforted me through lonely nights and kept me from committing suicide until I could seek professional help.

In the language of these stories, God's healing presence is not a cauterizing touch that burns away our layers of pain. Rather, it is an abiding love that bears witness to every tear.

[54]

One woman wrote powerfully about her discovery of this in-dwelling presence:

> I think the thing that was the most upsetting was that at the time I felt I needed to feel closeness to God the most, I felt that he was a stranger—in part because I was rethinking my definition of God. I found that the idea that was most helpful at that time was replacing my feeling of estrangement with an image from the popular writing called "Footsteps." Instead of visualizing myself all alone, abandoned by God, I tried to visualize myself as being so void of any spiritual reserves that all I could do was sit back or lay back and let God carry me through the situation. It was like the feeling of waking up from surgery and realizing that a loved one was in the room, not having the strength to carry on a conversation or possibly even recognize his or her presence, but being comforted by that knowledge.

In the middle of deep pain this feeling of presence may at first seem ineffectual. The stories of the divorced, however, suggest that through one's suffering, one comes to treasure the constancy of a love that endures and perceive that this love is a more profound gift than a momentary rescue in times of crisis.

The presence of God is an awakening agent. It prods us to examine ourselves and our world in more depth. Many who responded to the divorce questionnaire identified this quality of God in their lives:

> I started going to the United Church of Christ regularly and I found a sense of peace and support. I realized my life as it was—not happy. It was a lie. It took a great deal of soul-searching and prayer to realize that God understood the basis of our marriage was not truth, and that doubt was present from the beginning. I believe that God could understand the motives were good, even though I was not truthful with myself. The greatest task was forgiving myself.

* * *

Being in that marriage caused me to deny who I was to such a great extent that even now I have trouble knowing just who God made me to be. Sometimes I just can't get in touch with that. I conformed to so many societal, wife, mother expectations that I almost lost who I was. I am still sorting that out. I feel a great urgency about this task. It is so compelling that I am certain that this task is what I am born to do. . . . My immature faith was a major factor in my decision to marry Bob. I felt it was my Christian responsibility to help him. He was a good person who needed to be loved and cared for, so I married someone who needed me and whom I cared for, for the wrong reasons, rather than someone who was an equal person. Then I spent the major part of my married life trying to make things okay for us and him. It was partly due to my faith journey and coming to understand myself that I had to accept the reality that my motives were selfish and unwholesome and that I was standing in the way of God's work with Bob and that the relationship was in the way of my personal development to become who God wanted me to be. Therefore, to be honest, I had to leave the marriage. It was a matter of ethics.

*   *   *

I feel very strongly that God provided me with the people that I needed, when I needed them. My healing came from God. I had always had a strong belief in God, but the Bible, prayers, hymns, and sermons always meant someone else, not me. They didn't apply to me. I began to hear things with new ears and see things with new eyes. I had no faith in God, that He loved me or answered my prayers. I had always read the Bible and prayed, but with no conviction of faith that He would answer. After all the trauma of divorce, I began to apply the meanings of prayers, sermons, and hymns to myself and my life. I have developed a stronger faith in God. I know he loves me and will care for me if I let God do his work and let go of my own selfishness. He has brought me a very long way in the past five years, and I'm forever grateful to God. In retrospect, my first marriage was terrible and should have ended. I would never have had the courage to end it, so I'm glad Joe did. It was the kindest thing he could have done for me, although that wasn't his motive at the time.

The abiding presence of God acts in the lives of divorced Christians beneath the level of doctrine. It enables them to know that God is with them, accepting and valuing their life experiences, divorce notwithstanding. One woman put it this way in a letter to her friends:

> I separated in October, which began a period of darkness in my life unlike any I had ever known. It is difficult for me to reach out in the midst of an unwelcomed experience, but I don't want to lose touch with you, so I write this letter. I think, perhaps, the greatest challenge is for me to struggle to embrace fully my own humanity, to be alternately well and not well, to know that someday the panic and sadness will subside, but for now, at times, it must be.

In the church this subtle healing has not been as visible as it might have been because many Christians have been slow to perceive divorce as something other than a state of uncleanness. The stories of the divorced illustrate how frequently the death of a marriage makes those who are involved feel "unclean." It is a revealing phrase, rich in Old Testament symbolism. We find the term uncleanness to be contained within the Holiness Code given to the children of Israel by Yahweh. One of the main concerns of this code, which is found in Leviticus and in Deuteronomy, is to set forth standards that help the people to discriminate between righteous conduct and sinful conduct, between that which is clean and that which is unclean. In Leviticus we find this passage: "You are to distinguish between the holy and the common, and between the unclean and the clean; and you are to teach the people of Israel, all the statutes which the Lord has spoken to them by Moses [10:10]."

In this scheme of faith, uncleanliness is synonymous with estrangement from God and, in the words of *The Interpreter's*

[57]

Bible, "implies a kind of guilt." Although it seems archaic, there are still areas of life in which the church applies uncleanness standards today. True, we no longer follow the dietary laws as if they were the word of God nor feel that semen and menstrual blood are defilements of the Lord (Leviticus 15:16–31). We no longer sacrifice a year-old lamb and a turtledove to take away the uncleanness that accompanies childbirth (Leviticus 12). Yet we have, in many ways, surrounded the experience of divorce with a mystique of uncleanness. It is ironic because there were no associations of uncleanness attached to divorce in Old Testament Jewish culture. Nonetheless, the church has invited, and continues to invite, its divorced men and women to feel that they must atone for a sin. Lewis Rambo nicely identified this fact in his groundbreaking work *The Divorcing Christian:*

> Naturally, everybody feels guilty during divorce, but as Christians we have to bear not only the failure and family pressures of the divorce but also a strong sense that we've violated the strictures of the church and even of God. We may become suicidal with the hopeless feeling of having disobeyed God's will: I've done this horrible thing and there is no way to atone for the sins of the past; I'm miserably alone now, rejected by the church and my friends, and I'm damned for eternity because of my crime. If that sounds overstated for some of you, others from legalistic traditions will know the agony of a ruthless conscience that haunts every step of the way, and even invades our dreams to disrupt the fleeting moments of escape and refreshment sleep should bring.[32]

The church needs to ameliorate not encourage such feelings. It can do so by recognizing that divorced Christians have a vocation within the church. Perhaps the divorced are called by God, not to mourn in lonely exile, but to discover wisdom through their suffering. It is this possibility of discovering their vocation that leads divorced Christians beyond feelings of uncleanness to the discovery that they are loved by God as

[58]

they are, and that God wills their wellness and wholeness in the face of the death of their marriage. It cannot be said too strongly that divorced Christians need and deserve compassionate, healing ministry from the church, and to the extent that it is offered, the church fulfills its ministry.

Sadly, a significant factor in creating the neurotic guilt that divorced Christians feel is the church itself. Yet the church has continued to offer proclamations about the sinfulness of divorce while remaining *doctrinally* ineffectual about the place of God's love in the lives of those who suffer from broken marriages. The evidence is compelling in this regard. It is found both in the contemporary teachings of many denominations and in the stories of those many divorced Christians who were not supported by the church. Myrna and Robert Kysar's work *The Assundered: Biblical Teachings on Divorce and Remarriage* is a case in point:

> The New Testament presents us with a clear prohibition against divorce and remarriage, based on the divine intention for marriage expressed in Genesis 2. What has become clear is that the prohibition against divorce and remarriage roots in a vision of what God desires of marriage. . . . Marriage is a divine institution originated by God. The intention of that institution is that male and female realize a spiritual union. Therefore, the union visualized for marriage is an indissoluble kind. It is such a thorough merging of the two personalities into one life that disjunction is unimaginable. It is like the union of the ingredients for a cake. Once they are mixed together in the cake dough, it is inconceivable that they may once again be separated into their individual parts.[33]

The metaphor is lacking in depth. Although it reaches for an image of spiritual union, it neglects to dignify the individual lives of those involved. Those who marry do not completely lose their identity in the relationship, nor should they. While it is indeed true that there is a spiritual dimension of marriage in which people discover the experience of losing themselves in and for one another, it is also the case that healthy marriages must involve self-discovery and personal fulfillment. To suggest that married people should find contentment in the image of cake dough is hardly a noble vision of the spiritual power of marriage. It encourages people to submerge their own individuality and needs in the name of a greater whole, often with disastrous results. Women, in particular, have noted how this encouragement to submerge one's identity in marriage has violated their personhood to such an extent that it facilitated their divorce. As one woman wrote:

> The church played an integral part of awakening which led toward divorce. The exclusiveness of liturgy toward male domination supported my husband's demand for submission and his being "head." The church pressure for "oneness" was focused on the demand for my conformity to women's role as nurturer and supporter—but always behind men. The discounting and devaluing of women was modeled, and supported husband and family belief, that I was "wrong," "unstable," etc., etc., to desire freedom and a space to grow as led by God.

What, then, are we to say of God's place in marriage? In the first place, it seems accurate, as the Kysars suggest, to say that God hopes for people to lose themselves in a profound spiritual union. The Genesis 2 passage that images a husband and wife becoming "as one flesh" is profound and worthy of celebration. Yet it is equally important for the church to assert that God values an individual's search for authenticity and integrity and continues to love him or her even if that quest ends in divorce. The church needs to celebrate those nurturing marriages in which a husband and a wife can lay down their lives for each other, but it also needs to dignify the courage of a man or a woman who has risen again in the face of a marriage that has died. Such sensitivities are not just modern constructs; they are squarely within the tradition of the

[60]

church. Jesus' challenge for disciples to love him more than mother or father is a compelling ideal, but so is his willingness to feed Peter bread and fish at the Sea of Tiberias after Peter denied him. Jesus' gentle, forgiving question, "Simon, son of John, do you love me more than these?" is a poignant reminder that theological proclamations about the indissolubility of marriage are noisy gongs and clanging cymbals unless they are accompanied by equal affirmation that God loves divorced Christians as whole people of faith. As Richard Morgan noted in a 1982 *Christian Ministry* article titled "Any Balm in Gilead for Divorced Clergy?" the most serious failure of the church's position on divorce is its "unwillingness to view divorce and remarriage as acts of redemption and new beginnings."[34]

Such a perception is not often found in the doctrines or teachings of the church. The traditional Catholic approach to divorce, for instance, involves the use of ecclesiastical tribunals to discover authentic grounds for the annulment of a marriage or, alternatively, to offer a "restraining power that makes vocal the ideals that might otherwise be silenced."[35] Without formal ecclesiastical annulment, all remarriage is perceived by the church as a form of polygyny or polyandry. The Episcopal Church allows divorced members to secure permission from the bishop to remarry provided that they have been divorced for at least one year. The United Methodist Church prohibits remarriage except in cases in which one has been deceived by one's spouse through adultery or other wrongdoing involving deceit or immoral behavior. The United Lutheran Church in America asserts that marriage is indissoluble and permits remarriage through the patronizing justification that God's forgiveness of sinners leads God to provide for their needs. Finally, the United Presbyterian Church recognizes divorce only if the grounds for the separation are stated explicitly in scripture or implicitly in the New Testament. According to the Directory for Worship, Presby-

[61]

terian clergy can officiate in a second marriage only if the divorced bride or groom demonstrates remorse over past sins and promises this time to enter into a loving marriage for life.[36]

Such doctrines illustrate the church's negative emphasis in its ministry to the divorced. Many denominations have reserved the right to refuse to "recognize" the divorce of certain people, even though their pain and grief may be the same as those who, in the church's eyes, have been divorced legitimately. Moreover, the church has not always recognized the integrity of remarriage. For some denominations, a second marriage is nothing more than God's gracious love providing for sinners who justly deserve to be punished. For other denominations, a whole future after divorce is obtainable only if one shows remorse, a teaching that reminds divorced men and women that they are "failed" Christians who are of a lower caliber than those who have done the will of God by maintaining one continuous married relationship.

This patronizing perspective is even more overt when applied to the clergy. Many articles written since the 1970s have condemned clergy divorce in principle while ignoring the actual circumstances. For instance, Leigh Jordahl, in a 1975 article titled "On Clerical Divorce," argues that the essential role of clergy is to act as a "blameless" example for those in the parish: "If the divorce-remarriage epidemic among the clergy continues, the church will lose, and deserves to lose, even what strained credibility it still enjoys."[37] Jordahl concludes that all divorced clergy have an ethical responsibility to withdraw from public ministry. Although they are aggressively moralistic and emotional, Jordahl's arguments are not persuasive. This is the case on several grounds. First, there is great question as to whether it is the responsibility of clergy to be "blameless" examples for their congregations and even greater question as to whether such an ideal is meaningful.

To be sure, many have championed this thesis. Peter

[62]

Berger, for instance, was enlisted by Jordahl in his own defense. He affirms Berger's contention that "the minister is full-time Christian vicariously for those who manage to be Christian from time to time only."[38] Such images have a fatal flaw. They do not take seriously the doctrine of the priesthood of all believers, nor do they empower committed Christians to recognize their spiritual gifts and to grow in their ability to express them. Instead, they encourage the laity to be passive sheep who defer to the shepherd to direct them in appropriate ways and to live out the kind of ambitious witness that they themselves cannot quite manage. The pastor is to be the church for the laity, but a blameless pastor who serves as a vicarious hero or heroine for unempowered Christians inevitably substitutes a theocratic priesthood for koinonia.

There is an even deeper fallacy in such an understanding. In its desire to urge clergy to offer a blameless faith, this perspective denies the sinfulness of all people and God's propensity to use our sinfulness in the cause of the divine dream. It is a far more serious theological error to invite ministers to be blameless examples than it is to forgive their divorces. All clergy sin—in marriage as well as in divorce. Those who pretend otherwise chase illusions of perfection and ignore the ways in which God uses ambiguous humankind to make God's will manifest.

Were we more humble, we might better appreciate the paradox contained in the fact that Peter, the rock of the church, is blame personified and that Christ has always worked through the fallibility and woundedness of the clergy to create a church that loves, heals, and forgives people in spite of sins. We would then have the capacity responsibly to work through the pain of their divorce in the way that the following story details:

> My faith was deepened. God seemed very present, and I felt much more sure of my call. The concept of a God who suffers

with us took on great meaning for me. Prayer was very important—scripture reading less so. Worship (as an attending par-
ticipant) was often painful and frequently made me cry. I was
job hunting at the time. The church which eventually called
me said during the interview: "We don't mind that you're divorced. We just want to make sure it is finished so we don't
have to go through any of it."

At the same time, we would avoid unforgiving situations such
as these:

The sense that God loved me was more real than ever before;
that the people of God loved me was doubtful. God's actions
toward me seem to be incarnated largely from those "not of the
church." I found little in my faith or the church's ministry that
spoke to divorce in a positive way.

* * *

Despair and disappointment were the messages communicated to me by the liturgy, prayer, sermon, hymns, and
even the eucharist in the Missouri Synod church where I was
reared; I left it several years before the divorce and tried
another brand of Lutheranism and was only slightly less dis-
mal. The liturgy of Roman Catholicism was somehow healing,
but I never attempted contact with the clergy. Finally, my
pastor from Mount Olivet Baptist Church assured me of God's
abiding presence and that I was a person whom God loved.

Thankfully, we are entering a new era in ministry with the
divorced. It is a ministry, not of old-age moralizing, but of
new-age healing. It is a practicing of hospitality through
which the church finds ways to keep faith with divorced people and welcome them into community. A church that can
offer this kind of honest presence will find that it is providing
a significant witness to a significant group of people and is
deepening its own sense of community.

CHAPTER THREE

Of Samaritans and Slaves' Ears

The stories of the divorced make it clear that healing is significantly dependent on friendship. This gift of friendship is unpredictable, and it comes to the divorced in surprising ways. Friendships are a lifeline; they connect people who are filled with despair to the wider world. In some cases these lifelines of friendship seem providential. In other cases they are the evidence of people's kindness. Regardless of the particular perception, the most striking point to be made is that divorced people consistently tell of divorced friends who offered them compassion in the midst of overwhelming pain.

A friend is a wondrous thing. Joseph Addison has noted that friendship improves happiness and abates misery by "doubling our joy and dividing our grief." Friends, in other words, are those who share and transform our most memorable moments: our times of great satisfaction and our seasons of desolation. Friends laugh with us when life is sweet. They meet our eyes and gaze into them with an understanding that bubbles like a sparkling wine. Through such a look of friendship, the spirits of people dance together. Friendship also appears during our moments of despair and shares the weight of our pain. It scratches away the scab of defensiveness that covers a significant emotional injury and exposes the wound to the air. It invites us to open ourselves to the possibility of being healed by others. In these ways friends multiply and divide our grief. Clark Moustakas has suggested that it is the peculiar gift of friends to offer "a share" of their being. He notes the following insight from Marcel's work *The Mystery of Being:* "When somebody's presence does really make itself felt, it can refresh my inner being; it reveals me to myself, it makes me more fully myself than I should be if I were not exposed to its impact."[1]

Friendships that refresh our inner being have nothing to do with duration. Those who most profoundly share our laughter and our tears, our moments of marriage and divorce, may be long-term friends who have been our companions through many seasons. But often they are strangers who unpredictably provide us with a short-term, renewing presence.

I think of a friend who intensely entered my life in the middle of my divorce and proved to be an elixir. He was drawn by my pain and loneliness. This friend intuited my mood and merged with it. He invited me to spend time with him and a new network of friends. He encouraged me to share my feelings and received them with respect. He laughed with me and let me know I was a person worthy of friendship. He invited me to be happy with others and let me know that I had the right to be.

We have seen how profoundly divorce cripples one's presence in the world. After one's marriage ends, one is shy and tentative. One is afraid that old friends will disappear and that new ones will be disinterested. One worries that one can no longer be intimate with others. In the midst of such feelings, my friend's laughter, smile, and invitations to play a game of softball in Golden Gate Park forced me to confront these distortions within myself. His friendship led me to see that divorce does not destroy one's capacity for meaningful relationships.

All this happened unexpectedly. I was not a close friend of this man before my divorce and I did not spend a great deal of time with him in the years after. He came to me like a Samaritan on my road and healed me. In the words of Moustakas, he offered me a share of his being. Then he left San Francisco. Perhaps he returned to New York City or followed his dream of starting a community with friends in northern Idaho. It has been about fourteen years since I have seen this special friend, yet his memory is one of the sweetest and most compelling. If I had a day to spend with him, I'd broil a fat steak, pop the cork from a bottle of Beaujolais, and drink a toast for the healing he gave to me.

Other divorced people also speak with great appreciation of friends who helped them to heal. I received many comments like the following:

Friends were my major source of support. Two of the most sensitive men I know offered much—one by being an emotional prop and helping me to feel my own self-worth again after what I judged to be a great failure and the other by letting me talk it out without ever being judgmental about what I was saying. Two very special women were the basis of the rest of my support—one a college classmate with whom I have remained close and who was divorced and the other a clergy spouse who felt like a sister. Again, they most reassured me that I wasn't a bad person because my marriage didn't work out.

* * *

A few good friends, whom I had known for many years, kept calling to talk to me or, rather, to let me talk to them. They were concerned about me, asking what I had done for myself lately. Friends at work who invited me to do things also helped.

* * *

Former co-workers, a retired former pastor, my ex-wife's relatives, my Kiwanis friends: all of them let me know that they were with me, not against me. They sought me out and remained my friends. Even my ex-wife's sister did this and it meant a lot to me.

My best friend—a lady who works with me—was my best support. She offered me an ear to hear, a shoulder to cry on, and a hug. The lady friend I moved in with had been through the same thing and was very supportive. We had long discussions and I had lots of encouragement that I was not alone. But the most helpful person for me was a gentleman friend, two years divorced, who shared many hours of experiences and feelings with me and who listened for hours on end. He has moved from friend to dating partner, but not until three months of just being a friend.

* * *

The one person who was most directly helpful was a woman that I originally met through my church. I don't know if she did this of her own accord or at the suggestion of a church committee or the minister. For well over a year, she called me at least once a week and saw me regularly for lunch or invited me to dinner with her family. She even went to court with me. I was not much fun to be with at that time, and I guess I was surprised that someone would continue to call me and see me and ask how it was going when she knew she would just have to listen to more of my sadness and confusion. But she was always faithful when I couldn't reciprocate at all.

The last story contains some insightful understandings of healing friendship. It suggests that a friend is one who is able to flow with one's feelings in such a way that one is both understood and challenged. It also tells us that such healing is rarely instantaneous or dramatic. Rather, it is subtle and takes time. The account in the Gospel of John in which Mary anoints Jesus' feet with oil is an example of the way in which friendship heals the divorced. The anointing fixes nothing, resolves nothing, solves nothing. Rather, it is a loving caress that shares affection for its own sake. According to the text, Mary takes a pound of costly ointment and bathes Jesus' feet with it. So generously does she use the oil that the entire room is filled with its fragrance. Judas judges this display to be wasteful. He notes that the ointment cost 300 denarii, nearly a year's wages for one worker, and complains that the money should have been used to clothe and feed the poor. Jesus, however, commends this act of friendship and invites Judas to celebrate it by investing himself in it fully: "The poor you always have with you, but you do not always have me [John 12:8]."

The story is rich in symbolism. It sets before us the fact that simple acts of friendship contain a fragrance that can fill a house. It challenges us to accept that friendship does not have to do anything to be valuable. Friendship does not need to take away the pain of divorce, feed the hungry, or transcend the tragedy of the cross. Rather, friendship needs merely to be expressed lovingly. It is as simple as the pouring of oil on the feet of another and the wiping of them with one's hair. It is the gift of a massage that soothes away tension and pain. It is a compassionate touch without words that lets a troubled soul know that he or she is not alone.

Friendship is person-centered, not issue-centered. Those who touch us when we are in pain do so, not because they are committed to resolving a particular social problem, but because they have perceived another person who is burdened by tragedy and are moved to practice presence with them. Yet such friendships not only empathize with our pain, but also point beyond it. Both dimensions are essential. If friends only sympathize with our pain and mirror it back to us, friendship is reduced to sentimentality. If they only urge us to embrace visions that take little account of our actual life situation, the friendship seems moralistic and judgmental. True healing friendship begins with the experience of understanding another and accepting where he or she is, but it also involves a gentle clarifying process through which one who hurts is encouraged to see that there is life beyond one's grief.

This dual nature of friendship is expressed in two ways. The first we might call samaritanship. This mode of befriending

[69]

meets basic needs. The second we can call conceptual friendship. This style of relationship helps people to understand the dimensions of their grief. Several persons gave vivid accounts of samaritan-like friendships:

> My main source of support were my friends that I work sheep with and the people in my church. I was afraid that they would abandon me, or that the church would ask me to leave. Instead, they came through by loving in stronger ways than I could ever have expected. They took care of my kids. They gave me extra money. When I moved all the furniture out of the house to my ex-wife's apartment, people gave me what they could spare so that my children and I could still have some evidence of a home.

* * *

> I cannot ever forget the friends who stuck by me, especially the ones who also experienced divorce, the ones who lent me their husbands when my car didn't work and took care of my daughter when I worked or went out.

* * *

> My new pastor stayed in touch with me, was concerned not only for me but for my work. During a long hospitalization, he was a constant visitor and found a way to cover non-insured bills. He made enough of a contribution to keep me active in my annuity fund. As the divorce proceedings began, he used discretionary funds to pay my lawyer's fees, which I could not afford. He did not probe at all into the reasons for the divorce, my past, or my future. He was not a person I wanted to confide in as a counselor and he accepted that.

Others spoke of the ways in which conceptual friendships challenged them to understand the process of divorce more deeply and to move beyond guilt, anger, and pain to healing:

> One of the most hopeful experiences at the time of my divorce was the incredible amount of support and care given to me by

[70]

my friends in the seminary community and by the association minister who placed me as a camp director and really stood by me as I sought new directions for my life. The entire experience opened up a new world of trust, freedom, and honest sharing for me.

*   *   *

The major sources of support were my diaconate and leadership—several women and men in the parish in whose company I could cry and share my pain. I could be angry and swear. They accepted me. There were also some who held me. My people were beautiful!

*   *   *

My psychiatrist helped me to realize that I could cope, I could manage, that I was me, a person, not just part of an "us" that had died. I always had the feeling that I was living a book, page by page, and he had read the book before and knew just how it would end. But he never told me the ending; he just helped me to get through, chapter by chapter.

Friends, as we can see through these stories, provide diverse healing ministries to the divorced. On the one hand, they tend our wounds. On the other hand, they dialogue with us, hear us, and stretch our vision.

These images of friendship are important for divorced Christians to entertain, for they remind us that people are worthy of friendship and love, regardless of particular life circumstances. This aspect of worthiness is significant, for divorce radically alters one's social sphere, as the following stories point out:

I felt my "home" church and the local people should have been more supportive. That religious group, however, is so straight-laced that I guess I shouldn't even have expected it. Once I had gone away to school, I knew I just didn't fit there anymore. But the local "rejection" did hurt. Some former friends didn't want to be seen with me after the divorce—like I was "unclean." Basically, I learned to know who to avoid in asking for support. I knew how to avoid further rejection.

* * *

My friends, who I thought would support me, did not do so. My church did not do so either. We had been part of a close circle of married couples mostly from the church, and met frequently for social activities. Shortly after he moved out, I stopped being invited to the gatherings.

* * *

I felt the support of friends could have been stronger, but the married couples just turned their backs on me. They offered advice like, "Go have a few flings; if he can do it, so can you." To me that was awful advice, and I think they only enjoyed seeing me hurt. Many people felt that they needed to keep me up to date on my ex-husband's whereabouts, his girl friends, etc. For them, it was like having their own little "soap" series to watch.

It seems important to note how frequently divorced people are shunned by previous friends. Like the victim who is beaten and left on the road for dead, the divorced often watch men and women they thought they could count on walk by them like the priest and Levite. When an unknown friend stops, listens, understands, and cares, the relief is great. Loneliness is overcome. One feels like a worthwhile person again. Fortunately, this rejection by long-term friends is counterpointed by the fact that divorced people are also befriended in surprising ways. As we have seen, this befriending can occur through strangers. But it can also come through members of our family that we have taken for granted. A woman wrote about the friendship that came to her through family members that she assumed could never understand or accept her:

Initially, my support was through a few friends who supported my decision to seek professional counseling. I did not involve my family because of guilt and because of a personal resolve not to burden them with my problems. (I got myself into this; I'll have to get myself out. After all, they did not support my decision to marry this man.) Then a friend I worked with led me to a pastoral counseling service at the United Church of Christ. I started going to church and found myself unpredictably moved by the messages I heard. I made an appointment and talked with the pastor. It was after this decision that I decided to talk with my family and found that they welcomed me with open arms. They subsequently provided me with a tremendous amount of support. I found that the love I thought had waned had actually been waiting all along.

Divorce, then, is a relationship-changing event. It alters the constellation of one's family and one's friendships. It seems in fact that none of the relationships that are impacted by divorce remains the same. Old relationships are either renewed or turned to dust by the broken marriage. New friends either offer an unexpected understanding and compassion or turn their backs and refrain from getting involved. Two stories particularly illustrate the extremes of relationship-changing that so regularly accompany divorce. One woman shared the way in which her neighbors became more intimately involved in her life because of her divorce: "My major sources of support were my neighbors. After my husband left, these two neighbors called every single morning, and if I was depressed, they called at intervals throughout the day and evening." Another spoke of the isolation she felt from church and family.

I guess the main sources of support that were missing were the support of my parents and church friends. My friends at the church seemed to feel that because I initiated the divorce, regardless of the reasons, I was wrong. There were also other friends and family who took sides, and I felt very bad about some of those who had known me for years!

The friendships that surround the divorced transcend stylized categories and are unpredictable. There are reasons for this volatile character of friendship. Long-term friends often cannot remain close to a couple who divorces because they feel torn between two people they like. In addition there is a temptation on the part of long-term friends to assign blame rather than provide comfort. Our culture is peculiarly prone to pin failures, defeats, breakdowns, and estrangements on the responsible party, as if every tragic event in life is someone's fault. Certainly, the divorced have been disproportionately stereotyped and blamed in this way. And the blame has not been discriminating. As shown in the last story, the one who initiates divorce is often judged to be the guilty party. However, those who have been divorced are also often blamed. A man wrote:

> The source that hurt the most was my ex-wife's family. They had sort of shunned our family for years, forgotten the children's birthdays, Christmas, and other special times. They never came to visit us. Now that the divorce has happened, they are suddenly interested in the kids and in my ex-wife. Obviously, they had never accepted me. That hurt, and I resent their interference now very much, for they were not there to support our family during other years of struggle.

Long-term friends sometimes distance themselves because of their own discomfort over a situation that they cannot accept. A divorced man noted:

> Former "friends" and my own minister, whom I had worked hard with at church and socialized with, were not supportive at all. They felt I had "left my loyal wife of thirty-three years for a younger woman" and refused to consider my side of the situation.

[74]

Old friends can turn on the divorced and view their tragedy as a form of entertainment, as in the case of the woman who felt like a "soap." Another woman noted how long-term friends and family alienated her by wanting to hear the "juicy details."

> I was disappointed that my parents and some other relatives and friends could only seem to look at my situation in terms of how it affected them, not how it affected me. These people alternately wanted to hear all the "juicy details," which didn't really exist, or they didn't want to hear at all. I was surprised at some of the people who were willing to gossip about me.

Friends who provide an alternative to such antics are those who are, in the words of Thomas Dicken, gracious friends:

> A person is gracious when he or she does more than is required, goes beyond his or her duties, or does those duties in a gracious, rather than dutiful manner. . . . If people relate graciously, their concern for other persons is a gift, and gifts are free and spontaneous.[2]

We might say that friends of the divorced are those who go the second mile by responding gently, yet decisively, to those who are searching for ways to heal from the death of their primary relationship. The uniqueness of such friends lies in their ability to make themselves patiently accessible to divorced persons.

This gracious style of friendship manifests itself in several important ways. First, healing friendship in the life of a divorced woman or man is filled with a capacity to endure through contradictions and confusion. Friends of the divorced are not those who make order out of chaos; they are those who encourage the divorced to accept the contradictory nature of their lives. Such friendship is critical in our "ages and stages" culture, for we spend far too much time attempting to tame the mystery of life. Although it is true that such works as

[75]

Kübler-Ross' stages of death and dying, *Passages, The Seasons of a Man's Life, Between the Generations,* or *Stages of Faith* have offered many insights into the nature of human experience, it is also the case that they have invited us to conform to norms while overlooking the unpredictability of individual lives. It needs to be said that the divorced, as well as other people involved in major life transitions, need friends and counselors who honor their own unique rhythm and experience rather than pressure them to conform to the latest theory of human development. As one pastor noted:

> I found that the feeling stages of my divorce, as I expected, followed the dying process stages (Kübler-Ross). What I did not expect was the flopping about in these stages. I expected them to proceed in an orderly sequence and when you were through that was it. On the contrary, I would suddenly find myself back in a stage I thought I was through with.

Healing friendship during divorce gifts us with another who encourages us to resist the need for control and orderly sequence in an out-of-control time. Such friends refrain from offering us simplified schemas and solutions. Rather, they listen to us and understand us when we confess that we feel mad, depressed, or hopeless. They accept the fact that our emotions during a divorce reveal themselves in a kaleidoscopic manner, and they keep faith with us until we are able to reunify our lives.

Second, friends of the divorced are able to treat us as people among people. They recognize that divorce, as all-consuming as it might appear on the surface, does not constitute the whole of anyone's life, and they remind us of that fact. Such an awareness offers the divorced a critical gift of perspective even if the insight cannot be integrated at the time. At the same time, friends do not try to rescue others from the "disease" of singleness. Many divorced men and women said they felt great relief when they were finally treated as a person in their own right:

> It took a long time for friends to realize that they could invite me over without having a blind date for me in order to "round out the numbers."

* * *

> There were times when the last thing I wanted to hear was the word divorce. Those times may have been the most difficult for my friends to cope with because they expressed concern and I was totally unresponsive. Sometimes, I was "denying," but more often it was a healthy desire to have a life beyond divorce.

When new friends are not fixated on the trauma of one's recent divorce, healing can begin in earnest. Honest grief work is important to the healing process, but so are situations in which one's personal qualities are appreciated. One may happen to be a divorced teacher. Healing context depends not only on one's ability to work through one's feelings about the divorce, but also on friends who care more about one's gifts as a teacher than the fact that one is divorced. The point is this: Healing from divorce involves friends who can transcend the circumstances and categories of our lives and practice presence with us in the moment. Being in the moment may sometimes mean talking about the divorce experience, but it also involves entering into the other dimensions of a divorced person's life. Only in this way do the divorced regain their confidence and sense of worth.

Friends of the divorced, then, rip the label of "divorce" from men and women and relate to them as people. In so doing they overcome the anonymity that so often accompanies divorce. In too many cases the stigma of divorce has invited Christians to feel invisible. I recently attended a

[77]

meeting of a divorce support group that had been meeting for three years. The members recalled how isolated they had felt before the group was formed. They talked at length about the persistent feeling of invisibility they felt until their pastor, who happens to have experienced a divorce, specifically invited divorced people to a meeting. Twenty-five men and women showed up, and each was amazed to discover that she or he was not the only divorced person in the church. It was, for the members of the group, a liberating experience, a "coming out of the closet" that encouraged them to escape from the anonymity that had confined them, reclaim visibility by naming their life experience, and feel a sense of purpose, rather than failure, in that experience.

If the church wishes to offer a consistent healing ministry with the divorced, it needs to break through the stigma of divorce and the feelings of invisibility that flow from it. It needs to heal people as Jesus healed the ear of an anonymous slave. During the betrayal of Christ in the Garden of Gethsemane, the most obscure person is the slave of the high priest. The slave is a man caught in the middle. He has no power to influence the outcome of the drama that envelops him. Like many divorced Christians, he is held captive by events that he cannot control. When the followers of Jesus saw that the crowd was there to arrest Jesus, their first inclination was to resist with armed might. One screamed, "Lord, shall we strike with the sword?" Another drew his blade and cut off the ear of the slave. But Jesus said, "No more of this!" and he touched the wound and healed it (Luke 22:51).

Healing in the Christian tradition is most poignant when it touches the lives of the invisible and the anonymous. In the drama of the Garden of Gethsemane, Jesus reaches beyond the category of "slave" to find an injured person and heal him or her. We are called to do the same with the label "divorced." True, friends of the divorced generally do not offer this kind of miraculous healing, but this is not the essential point. What is at issue is the fact that authentic befriending of the divorced, like Jesus' befriending of the slave, depends on the church's ability to cut through a social category that isolates and touch the severed parts of those whose marriage has ended. This touching will often be subtle. We should expect that it will take time for healing to occur. We must cultivate the kind of enduring samaritanship that waits until the rhythms of healing assert themselves. If we can develop this sensitivity, we shall discover that our friendship is encouraging the divorced toward wholeness as surely, if more slowly, as Christ healed the ear of the unnamed slave.

CHAPTER FOUR

Of Sanctuaries and Inns
Without Rooms

The experience of the divorced within the church is highly ambiguous. As noted in chapter two, the church's theology of marriage and divorce has been inconsistent. On the one hand, the church has set forth a shifting doctrine of marriage that has alternately portrayed it as a gift from God and as a distraction to full relationship with God. On the other hand, the church has offered a theology of divorce that has both advocated divorce as a pathway to the religious life and condemned it as a mortal sin.

It should come as no surprise to discover that, in terms of their treatment by the church, the experiences of divorcing Christians vary widely. Significant numbers of those who responded to the questionnaire felt unsupported, judged, and shunned by their communities. At the same time, many others wrote with great gratitude of the healing ministry that their churches offered to them.

What factors distinguish rejection from acceptance? If we wish to offer a ministry that heals, we must know something about the ways in which the divorced feel empowered by the church as well as the ways in which they were invited to feel inadequate. I want to begin by analyzing the stories of those who did not find their churches helpful. Of the accounts I received, a minority of divorced men and women felt alienated by their churches. Nonetheless, their stories are significant, for they illuminate the ways in which the church continues to act as if there is "no room in the inn" when lonely, tired travelers ask for sanctuary and hope. One group of divorced people shared the conviction that their churches were confused about how to relate to divorced women and men:

> My church didn't know what to do with divorcing people (I didn't quite know what to do with them either!).

* * *

> The parish I was serving at the time of the breakup of my marriage was unable to minister to my wife or me. I became a non-person to them and for the great part have been ignored.

* * *

> The local church was not much help because of divided feelings of allegiance. After all, we were both very active members, and the message we both received was "Why have you messed this all up and made us feel so uncomfortable?"

Such stories identify the church's "sins" of omission. They remind us that many congregations are unable to cut through the stigma of divorce and touch people in compassionate ways. Embarrassment, anxiety, and lack of knowledge about how to respond lead many Christians to withdraw from the divorced.

On a related level, churches are almost exclusively family-centered in their emphasis, making it difficult for singles— particularly divorced men and women—to feel that there is a space which recognizes and potentiates their life situations. Indeed, a consistent response from divorced Christians who did not feel supported by their congregations was that the church was so focused on traditional, nuclear-family modes of ministry that it was unable to provide alternatives:

[81]

The church transmits a "coupled," Ark feeling so singles have to be very confident to mingle freely.

* * *

The most difficult or unhelpful thing was the total emphasis on "family" in church services, activities, reading materials, etc. And just adding the phrase "or single parent" after talking on and on about the family seems like tokenism. My experience is that a single, childless person has very different needs, problems, and joys from either traditional nuclear families or single-parent families. My church has recently been trying to respond better to the needs of divorced single parents, but I have been automatically lumped in with this group, which I don't feel a part of.

Others noted that the image provided in worship and sermons too often excludes singles—particularly divorced women and men:

I still have a hard time with some sermons, especially on Mother's Day. There is so much home and family emphasis, and so much of the worship is still based on the old nuclear family. Although Jesus accepted the prostitute, the adulteress, and those who were married again, I don't think much of that is preached. Maybe it's society's hangup on sex. We always hear about the prodigal son and his acceptance.

* * *

My church was of little help. Looking back, I can see that part of that was my responsibility. I had trouble sitting in church alone while everyone else was there with a spouse, shoulder to shoulder. My eyes could not see the widowed family/couple focus. Scriptures and sermons increased my guilt and depression. My pastor at the time made *no* acknowledgment of separation and divorce. (He had been an admirer of my husband for professional reasons.) I often left services early to keep from crying. Acquaintances at church asked me where my husband was, and I could not answer truthfully. It was a long time before I could tell them that we were separated. For three years I did not attend church.

Such experiences lead divorcing Christians to feel isolated and lonely. Their response is to turn to the spiritual dimensions of relationship with God rather than to the warmth of a caring community:

I was concerned about my divorce because I was married in church. I attended a church service of a friend of mine. The service was completely on church and divorce and what the Bible says about divorce. Unfortunately, a lot of things seemed dry or disappointing. I was not a real active churchgoer during divorce, but God definitely helped me through. I prayed a lot.

* * *

Now I know that whatever help I get from Christianity will be from the spiritual aspects, since the church is closing off to me. I am, of course, cutting myself off rather than being cut out, but it comes to the same. I have begun to pray for strength and courage, for peace and help out of the morass. I am feeling alone and cut off, with nowhere to go. Perhaps that's the beginning of faith—or the end. Who knows?

* * *

The one strong feeling I had at that time, and still do, is that churches are places for "complete families." I have many friends in the church, but I always feel alone. I cannot make myself join choir or teach Sunday school anymore. I absolutely cannot explain why I feel this way, but deep down it is the only place in my life where I feel "different."

Given such feelings, it would seem that one of the most relevant things the church can do is to soul-search with the divorced rather than programming for them. What is needed is faith-sharing that breaks through experiences of alienation, invisibility, and anonymity. Soul-searching encourages people to emote: to name their life space, to celebrate that which is good in it, and to confess their fears. It is the medium through which the church creates inclusive worship and frees people to encounter one another beneath such stereotypes as "divorced," "singles," and "widowers." Where this spirit of soul-searching is alive, divorced Christians and others who do not feel part of the Body of Christ can be reconciled to community.

Conversely, soul-searching cannot occur when judgments block the sharing of selves. Unfortunately, a significant number of divorced men and women have been judged, rather than understood, by their churches. Many noted the ways in which they were whipped by doctrine or reminded of the sinfulness of divorce. In such cases guilt was intensified and feelings of inadequacy magnified. A few Christians felt that they needed this kind of correction:

> Not long after our separation, the lectionary reading on divorce came up in the lectionary for preaching. I decided to go ahead and preach on the passage and attempted to tackle the divorce issue straight on in light of scripture. In essence, my sermon said that divorce is a sin. That is what broken covenants are, and there is no sense in trying to explain it away or justifying it. More important, however, is that Jesus forgives sins, and divorce is just one of the many he forgives. My Christian faith played the most significant role in my divorce. It was because of my Christian faith that my sense of failure was most acute, which I don't feel was necessarily bad, but even helpful in the long run.

* * *

> I wanted to hear sermons that told me I was doing wrong as well as those that patted my shoulder.

Far more responders, however, experienced judgments by the church as being guilt-producing and unhelpful:

> I didn't tell you my story so you would feel sorry for me. I don't want to convince you or anyone else that I did what God

wanted me to do. I'm not quoting the Bible or trying to say that divorce is "right." I only believe that if the people around me really thought I was doing something against God and against God's wishes that, yes, it was their duty to talk with me about it. Yes, we all fall and need to be reminded. But if I choose not to listen, the way to "win me back into the fold" is not to turn your back and give up on me, but to show me love and perhaps through your good example help to show me the way.

* * *

At first, I think being a Christian created the horrible guilt. If I didn't believe in marriage as a Christian institution with its vows of "till death do us part," I would not have felt condemned. Sermons still help me to feel guilty. What did divorce mean when the Bible was written and what does it mean today? I don't know. Even though I feel God is forgiving and loves us as we are, I know I haven't measured up to what a good Christian should be. There is still guilt—maybe that's good. . . . The hymn "Just as I Am" is my favorite, but it hurts the most. The Confession is especially important to me because I feel so inadequate in God's view. Interesting that I need to say the Confession and sometimes don't even "hear" the Assurance. Yet I know that God loves me. . . . Until five years ago I think I felt I was not worthy of anyone's love. My son and parents "had" to love me—it was part of their responsibility. It wasn't until I got married again that I felt someone loved me for me—with all my sins.

* * *

I still feel the church has this huge void in it when it comes to dealing with single-parent families. Traditionally, it has always been "mom and dad." It just isn't so anymore, and I strongly feel that if the church is going to survive it has to address this problem. I think the church has to attract more of the people who have gone through divorce. One of the major problems for me has been the lack of other people in my church to talk with who have had the same problem. I sometimes resent the feel-

[85]

ing that because you've had this happen, you're somehow doomed! Broken family and all that rot. My three-member family may have more going for it than the traditional nuclear family that is beset with lots of problems that have never been dealt with honestly. Naturally, my situation isn't one that anyone would choose, but it doesn't mean that my children don't have a chance to grow up healthy and happy. If I've learned anything, it's that there are no guarantees. I just have to try my best. I hope it's good enough.

Others offered a conceptual analysis. Several divorced men and women analyzed the ways in which they felt that the church exaggerates the value of commitment. One woman wrote, after she sought out her pastor for counseling, that she was encouraged to "stay together no matter what." Another observed:

> The least helpful thing for me was the concepts that were expressed about commitment. Even though these comments sometimes struck me as a grim determination, if not perseveration, I still felt guilty that I had broken this large Christian commitment.

Doctrinal absolutism sometimes works against itself. In the best sense, doctrines of faith have the power to lead us beyond what "is" to what "might be." Profound doctrine is the stuff of divine dreams and visions that call us to attempt a great way of life. They invite us to live for a purpose beyond ourselves and encourage us to stretch toward a wholeness that is greater than the status quo.

But when profound becomes unforgiving, it leads to perpetual dissatisfaction and guilt. The doctrine of the indissolubility of marriage, for instance, can invite divorced Christians to feel as if they have committed a crime against God, regardless of the realities of their former marriage. In the most extreme sense such invitations create frozen guilt in the lives of the divorced Christian, so that one must struggle to experi-

[86]

ence the forgiveness of God, even if one believes that such forgiveness is offered freely:

> I still struggle with guilt. I still wonder whether I've done the right thing. All I can say is that I've made my choice, and after much reflection and prayer I finally believe that God has accepted what I've done, right or wrong. God is forgiving, and if divorce is against God's will, I have asked forgiveness and God has given it to me as promised. I look at my present husband and the happiness that we have brought each other, and I ask, Have I really done so wrong?

Unyielding doctrine also has ambiguous effects on a congregation. Genuine doctrine cultivates a yearning for deeper unity with God's intention for human life. It inspires peope of faith to live in a way that connects them with the flow of creation. False doctrine, however, harps on "shoulds" and "oughts." Rather than inviting through the opportunity of healing, transfiguring faith, it punishes with the club of the law. Rather than sharing the gospel in a way that touches the heart, false doctrine parrots absolutes that bludgeon the intellect with charges of inadequacy. Thus, the next-to-last story characterized the church as "perseverating" about commitment, that is, as compulsively repeating doctrine without "the ability to shift easily to another at a change in stimulus."[1] Theological perseveration is characteristic of the behavior of the Pharisees who, in the words of Christ, laid heavy burdens of doctrine on the backs of the people while doing nothing to empower them to live more fully in the community of God. The church of our day has more work to do in creating a flexible ministry with the divorced that decisively leads them through a wilderness of guilt and grief to a promised land in which they can forever shed their feelings of failure and inadequacy. Such a ministry must be one that freely heals and resurrects the broken-hearted. It is one that must reflect God's own desire for renewal as portrayed in Revelation 21:3–4:

Behold, the dwelling place of God is with persons. God will dwell with them, and they shall be God's people, and God will be with them. God will wipe away the tear from every eye, and death shall be no more, neither shall there be mourning, nor crying, nor pain any more for the former things have passed away.

Divorced pastors offered an additional criticism of the church. A significant number of those who responded to the questionnaire noted that they were judged punitively by either local congregations or the church hierarchy:

> While both my association and my conference minister were supportive, this was not the case at churches where I interviewed for a job. Senior pastors (men) were particularly "concerned" over my recent divorce. I became tempted not to tell committees that I was divorced but did not do this, as to do so seemed deceiving. I was amazed at the insensitivity of senior pastors as I interviewed. I was asked many painful questions with judgmental attitudes.

* * *

> I think I had more support than most persons in such situations. One area, however, seemed immediately absent. After our church voted two to one to keep me as their minister, a pastor friend from out of state called to warn me that the conference leadership would want me to move and that I needed to be aware not to trust them. He said they were interested only in keeping as many dollars coming into the conference as possible. I was expendable. His call came a week after the conference minister sent me a letter, saying that I didn't want to stay with that kind of vote. I shared that letter with my leadership. They were offended and angry, and part of their anger eventually involved cutting financial support for the conference.
>
> In my view, the conference is very interested in keeping the dollars rolling in. They all seem to be under pressure from some place upstairs to keep producing more dollars for the Big

Church Program. They must get torn between loyalty to that program and loyalty to human beings who are pastors. Ultimately, they cannot serve both masters. After pastoring for thirty-five years my experience is that the conference generally tends to sell out the pastor, and even the church, for the dollars. While they are very professional and very sincere about their loyalty to our larger institutional truth, they are most concerned about furthering their own careers. I think this is a very human and very important limitation of the system.

* * *

My divorce has had a negative effect upon my potential for placement in ministry but a positive effect upon my compassion as a minister.

* * *

The conference office and staff totally ignored me, with the one exception of a support staff woman who was a personal friend. They never acknowledged my leaving the parish, my separation, or my unemployment. I sought placement help from the proper staff person and never heard from him again.

* * *

I hope you include a section on specific training on ministry with the divorced for conference staff. Our conference minister was almost no help at all and didn't seem to know how to proceed.

Such are the negative experiences of divorcing Christians who did not receive a compassionate response from the church. But there are many positive experiences as well. In fact, the majority of responses that I received *celebrated* the place of the church in the process of divorce.

Those who experienced the church as a healing community emphasized three ways in which the healing occurred: place, people, and pastor. Many divorced people portrayed the church as a place in which to cry or sing their pain. Others shared the experience of surrendering to their grief in a safe sanctuary and opening themselves to forgiveness. Some stories of this type are considered in the second chapter, but there are many more:

The church was a place for me to sit in prayer on Sunday and simply share my feelings. I found prayer most helpful. The hymns were very hard for me. My emotional level was extremely high. I was on the brink of tears in church very often and yet I wanted to be there. I felt a refuge in my church.

* * *

My church allowed me to be there and have meaning in a personal way. I went to church and cried silently through a lot of services.

* * *

I found my way back to church after being invited to attend a service with a friend. I felt that prayer, the scriptures, and some of the sermons were very helpful. I felt like I was a new person when I became involved with the church that I am currently attending. I felt like I had come "home" at last, and all the turmoil and trouble were past!

* * *

My Christian faith has always been the stabilizing force in my life for as long as I can remember. It kept me married for thirteen years when realistically the marriage probably should have ended long before that. I still had that faith during the divorce, but it became weaker or stronger, depending on where I was at. The guilt, the anger, the frustration nearly robbed me of it, and yes, it was dry and disappointing, but that was my faulty perception, my inability to forgive myself, my forsaking the faith, not God forsaking me. After all, I had always considered myself a basically good, loving, caring person. Yet here I was divorcing, which was saying, "I can't, or won't, love anymore."

[90]

I questioned whether I had any Christian faith at all. But I continued to go to church faithfully, even when I wasn't feeling very faithful. Just knowing that it was there and was a refuge from the pain I was feeling, a place where I wouldn't be turned away no matter how unworthy I felt, was encouraging. I was feeling very unworthy of my Christian faith because of the guilt I felt. But I continued to go to church as it was a haven from the hurt. I felt comforted there. I love music and must confess that out of everything in the service, it was the music which would reach my soul, comfort me, and often—even to this day—bring tears to my eyes or send a chill down my spine. Our minister always says, "I hope there is some part of this service that will reach out and touch you and the particular condition of your life this day." That always happened; it was either a hymn, something from scripture, or something in his sermon that inwardly made me cry out, "Yes, that's how I feel, that's where I'm at today." I knew if I continued to sit in that church Sunday after Sunday that I would eventually forgive myself and regain my faith as God had always forgiven me.

This sensitive perspective points out that much of the healing power of the church lies in its ability to provide relevant proclamation to divorcing Christians. Those who were healed in the church consistently wrote about the ways that the word of God spoke to them in worship:

I often went to church not having shared a new struggle and left with the feeling that my minister was clairvoyant and had been speaking straight to me.

* * *

There was a period of over a year where every church service seemed to be totally directed at me. Tears flowed even though I tried not to cry.

* * *

It's hard not to relate to prayers, scripture, sermons, and the messages they have whether because of divorce or some other everyday experience. How many times have I found myself

[91]

asking, "Is he talking to me?" when our pastor gives his sermon.

If one reflects on these accounts, it becomes clear that worship works its own mysterious will and way in the lives of suffering people. Through liturgy, divorcing Christians are able to work through feelings of inadequacy in order to feel God's forgiving love. Those who have had this experience point out that they were moved in unpredictable ways by a variety of elements of the liturgy, including prayer, music, scripture, and the eucharist. Each component of the liturgy seems to renew the divorced in its own unique way. Moreover, people are affected in their own special ways. Each is transformed by an encounter with specific elements of ritual. These encounters are sacred moments, like Jacob's wrestling match with an angel. They fill people with the "fear and trembling" that divine encounter always entails, as in the following account:

> I remember the first time I took communion after our separation. I sat in the church and cried the entire time, almost to the point of sobbing, and as hard as I tried to regain control, I couldn't. I wanted to get out of there but was in the middle of the church and felt I couldn't leave without making even more of a spectacle of myself. I was embarrassed but truly hurting as well. I felt unworthy to be sitting there partaking of this sacred rite because I felt I had failed not only myself, but Christ as well. As I take communion now, I often think back to that day and thank God for unendingly and unconditionally loving me.

Others were moved not so much by the place of the church as by the people within it. In such cases the community surrounded the divorced person with a sense of understanding, acceptance, and love. Depending on the congregation, the friendship expressed was both overt and subtle, but in either case it had the quality of koinonia—the gathered Body of believers who are prepared to suffer and celebrate together.

One woman shared the way in which the people of her community quietly supported her:

> As far as the members of the church are concerned, no one has said anything to me about my divorce. It's one of those things you just don't talk about in our small town, except as gossip. And I'd rather not talk about it anymore after all this time. There are more interesting and happier things to talk about. I've paid the price and hurt too long already.

*   *   *

> We have a warm and friendly congregation. Many told me to call any time just to talk or to visit if I felt like crying.

*   *   *

> Basically, the people of the congregation related to me the same, other than an added concern over my divorce. They offered to help and expressed their concern. I felt loved and cared for, and very much "a part."

*   *   *

> A big source of comfort and affirmation was my home congregation. They wouldn't let me drown in self-pity; they affirmed and challenged me to use my gifts. Healing and wholeness were constantly surrounding me.

*   *   *

> The church was one of the hardest places to go and tell people we were divorcing because the church was such a "couple's place," a place where family was valued and I was breaking up the family unit. After I told a few people, I was amazed at the responses. Most people were supportive. Some offered money, help with moving, kind words, etc.

The people of a church who offer the most profound support do so by walking with others through the pain that makes them hurt. It is often difficult to find a group of people who are able to support one another in this way. As one man said:

[93]

The support mechanism (whatever that might have been) was nearly nonexistent. Not always because I shunned it, but because I could not find it. There were many close to me who cared a great deal. They hurt because I hurt, cried because I cried, and wanted always to wave that magic wand and "make things better." But that was never reality.

The unique healing function of the Christian community is not that it magically makes things better, but that it provides us with an opportunity to share the ambiguous reality of our lives with one another. Parker Palmer notes, in his work *To Know as We Are Known,* that "we hide from the transforming power of truth; we evade truth's quest for us."[2] Much of truth's quest has to do with encountering others who perceive our suffering, reflect with us honestly and compassionately about the reasons for our pain, and encourage us to renew our life space.

The church as healing community encourages us to be pursued by truth precisely because it supports us in pondering the life conditions that are before us, rather than preaching to us of absolutes. Thus a healing community heightens our sensitivity to the moment and calls us to be accountable to the reality of our lives.

American culture excels at leading people into the moment through the pursuit of pleasure. We know how to lose ourselves in ecstasy but have great difficulty learning from our woundedness. Thomas Merton has suggested that it is the distinctive function of the community of faith to encourage people to find God in their moments of brokenness and to face their pain. The church, in other words, is one of the few institutions in our society that offers an alternative to the avoidance of the tragic moments of our lives. As Merton puts it:

The victory of monastic humility is the full acceptance of God's hidden action in the weakness and ordinariness and unsatisfactoriness of our own everyday lives. It is the acceptance of our incompleteness in order that He may make us complete in His own way.[3]

Churches that pursue this quality of monastic humility are able to accept human incompleteness. They are communities that are prepared to accept the reality of divorce within the lives of Christian men and women. Such congregations are less concerned with the tragedy of broken relationships than they are with the transfiguring power of God in human lives. They are therefore able to accept the divorced with full recognition of their "ordinariness and unsatisfactoriness."

The third area of support for the divorced is pastoral presence. Divorced Christians who responded to the questionnaire said that healing ministers were sensitive to pain and suffering, willing to listen in a compassionate and nonjudgmental way, and able to remind them of God's love during a time in which they felt hopelessly inadequate and undeserving:

My pastor was a great help because he had experienced loss and pain. He was the only pastor who understood and helped. We had many close UCC pastor friends because my husband was active in the church all his life. But it seemed that these other pastors turned their backs and said, "I'm sorry, but I don't know what to do."

* * *

When I went to the pastor to ask for help, I really wanted him to tell me that I needed to stay in my marriage, make it work, etc., etc. But he didn't. He asked me to see how my children and I could be destroyed. I knew he was right at a head level, but I had a terrible adjustment at the love level. I waited one and a half years before going ahead with the divorce.

* * *

Realizing that people in the church wanted to be my friend was most helpful, and best of all, the Singles Camp in my confer-

[95]

ence had its first session just when I needed help the most. The program seemed to have been developed for every need I had, with a clergy couple leading it. The support I received from new friends I met there was just what I needed. Seeing that they had come through the same kind of heartbreak I had and had coped so well and had found joy in life again was an inspiration.

* * *

The first winter of my divorce I joined a Bible study which allowed me to be close to a small group, even though we didn't discuss divorce. The minister who led the group helped me over the "sinful" feelings about getting divorced.

* * *

Mostly, I think, the two messages that kept coming through time and time again were that I am loved no matter what and that I am forgiven.

* * *

Joining and attending my "new church" was one of the most rewarding experiences of my life. I received strength from every hymn, every sermon, and all of the activities of the church. My pastor is a jewel and many of his sermons, I feel, were written just for me. I thank God for the church, the pastor, and the members.

* * *

The pastor often says a prayer for marriages that are breaking or have broken up. She encourages the congregation to accept divorce as a fact of life if it has to be and not to treat people as sinners—to be understanding and supportive.

* * *

My pastor seems to focus a great deal on relationships, and so there were many times that the scriptures, the sermons, and the prayers were especially helpful to issues that I was going through.

The church was helpful in many ways. First, our minister was always there with concern and comfort. The church services were empowering, just the feeling of being closer to God and gathering strength to carry on through next week.

* * *

Because my pastor made it a point to bring divorce into the open at church, I never felt uncomfortable. For a couple of months after my separation, I always felt as if at least one prayer, hymn, or sermon would apply to me. I was eventually made to feel accepted as part of the community, and that is what I'm struggling not to lose now.

In all cases, pastors who practice compassionate ministry are those who show respect, identify the life space of those who are divorced, listen, and offer compassion. In few cases did divorced Christians feel empowered by pastors who judged, called for penance, or criticized. On the contrary, divorced Christians who maintained a relationship with their community did so because the church offered kindness and encouraged them to heal. When the pastors offer such a ministry, those who have suffered through a divorce express great gratitude.

The implication of these accounts is unmistakable: Divorced Christians who remain in community are those who receive a compassionate response from people in their congregation, an insightful ministry from their pastor, or a sanctuary within which to participate in healing liturgy.

Divorced men and women have at least three lessons to offer the church. The first is to remind the church that judgment without love does not provide a context for healing ministry. The divorced teach us that when we overplay our confessional hand, we alienate the very people we hope to heal, serve, and save. In turn, this insight leads us to consider that the practice of compassionate ministry calls pastors to offer forgiveness *before* judging or expecting confession.

The accounts of the divorced, to say nothing of the accounts of healing in the New Testament, demonstrate that those who are healed of heartache are those who are first assured that they are loved and have the power to take up their bed and walk. This is the kind of acceptance and assurance that the church is called to offer to those who suffer from broken marriages. Where such compassion is offered, the church's proclamation of God's forgiving love takes on real meaning, and the authority of the church is inevitably deepened.

The second thing that the divorced have to teach the church is that love is the greatest of powers. Through the centuries the church has studiously avoided offering too much love too quickly. When the errant come to the church with their pain, guilt, and feelings of sinfulness, the church has assumed that confession is better for the soul than forgiving love. As a result, the church has too often withheld its greatest strength—the ability to help the divorced recover a sense that God loves them and that they are valuable people.

Full acceptance of the divorced has been slow to occur because many Christians have insisted that compassion without judgment encourages permissiveness in marriage. Others have suggested that unless the church firmly calls those who have divorced to repentance, the church's standards will be irreparably compromised.

In the face of such concerns the divorced challenge Christians to consider that love is not as ineffectual as is sometimes assumed. They encourage us to reflect on the fact that far from being a means of cheap grace, compassionate love is the force that renews lives. Indeed, the more the church becomes a community that embraces those whose lives are burdened by pain and failure, the more we are all empowered to examine the hurts of our lives and to heal. What the church needs to do most, in terms of ministry with the divorced, is to increase its trust in this power of healing love by practicing restraint in confronting the divorced with their failures while offering a space in which they can unburden themselves because they have first known that they are loved.

The third thing that the divorced have to teach the church is that healing ministry with the divorced is an authentic form of ministry waiting to be developed. Statistically, the divorced constitute a significant proportion of the population in both the church and the culture-at-large. Nearly half of all marriages end in divorce. The average marriage lasts 6.8 years. By any yardstick, the church is confronted with a large group of people with tangible hurts to whom it is invited to offer compassion. It is one more case of the harvest being plentiful and the laborers few. If the church were to marshal its healing resources and embrace these men and women, it would discover that it is not only offering healing, but also finding a new integrity and sense of satisfaction in its work.

So often the church spins its wheels by worrying about whether to become involved in a particular ministry. At the same time, Christians feel frustrated because new people do not come to the church. In the midst of such stalemates the divorced can teach the church that it needs to turn its attention to those places where it is not offering caring witness. The area of divorce is precisely such an area.

The divorced encourage the church to consider that there is creative ministry to be done if only we can outgrow the need to judge those whose life decisions are different from what we think they should be, listen to those who suffer, and offer them a liberating response.

Perhaps what is needed is a ministry with the divorced that incorporates Jesus' commissioning of the seventy. Jesus sends these people to minister in teams of two. The spirit of this ministry is to heal and to preach God's grace to those who have need. As the Gospel of Luke says, "Whatever house you enter, first say, 'Peace be to this house!'. . . Whenever you enter a town and they receive you, eat what is set before you; heal the sick in it and say to them, 'The kingdom of God has come near to you. [Luke 10:5, 8–9].' "

No conditions are placed on the offering of this ministry other than that people be open to the sharing of the good news and the touch that heals. Jesus does not ask that people live or behave a particular way in order to be healed. All he asks is that people respond to the Word of God that is preached. Similarly, in his own ministry, he heals by inviting the lame to pick up their beds and walk without first asking for repentance.

This is a significant lesson to ponder when considering the role of the church in the lives of the divorced, for the church has been too miserly in its compassion for the divorced, preferring to withhold it until penance has been performed. But nowhere in the sending out of ministers into the world does Christ ask them to be concerned about effecting repentance before offering healing. Just the opposite is the case: In the sending out of the seventy, ministry is offered unconditionally and freely. No judgment is placed on the life circumstances of those who are served. This is the kind of prophetic ministry that the church needs to offer to the divorced. For too long the church has grumbled about the sinfulness of divorce, decried the breakup of God's ordained plan for the nuclear family, and felt that it must judge divorced Christians in order to bear witness to God's dream of perfect commitment. But such proclamations are reactive. They complain about the reality of human community, rather than seeking to transform and heal it. To break this reactive pattern of ministry with the divorced we must open ourselves to Christ, who commissions us to go to the house of the brokenhearted, the lonely, and the grieving. There we are to say, "Peace be to this house!" and we are to heal the injuries that accompany divorce. If we can do this, we will be offering an entirely new ministry to the divorced, and we will learn to deepen our own trust in the power of healing love.

CHAPTER FIVE

"Go and Sin No More"

We have seen that the church's ministry with the divorced is ambiguous. On the one hand, the assurance of God's forgiveness has so often been accompanied by invitations to feel remorseful and guilty that many divorced Christians have never experienced God's love for them, nor have they been able to accept themselves as whole people, worthy of love. On the other hand, many divorced women and men have been comforted, empowered, and healed by the church.

We must conclude that the church's ministry with the divorced is one that peers through a glass dimly rather than communing face to face. What is needed is a more decisive ministry, one which recognizes that the ability to accept divorced Christians as whole people of God is at the heart of Christian theology. To pursue this quest for a more decisive ministry, three significant questions need to be addressed: First, what is the shape of a healing theology of divorce? Second, is divorce inevitably a sin? Third, what is authentic forgiveness?

A theology of divorce begins with the recognition that divorce is, most fundamentally, the death of relationship. This death does not necessarily involve moral failure, nor is it necessarily unhealthy. It is, however, inevitably tragic because divorce involves great pain and loneliness. One woman said that she could physically feel her heart tear during her divorce, and another said, "I felt my life was over, like the words from a Kenny Rogers song: 'the best thing that could happen is to die in my sleep.'"

We have spent a great deal of time listening to divorced Christians, and if we have heard them in a sensitive way, we can only be humbled by the depth of grief that lies beneath all conjecture about whether or not divorce is a violation of God's intent for human relationships. A theology of divorce, then, grows out of the woundedness of human relationships.

When theology attempts, conceptually, to portray God's intention for marriage, it must, as an essential part of its discipline, ground its interpretation of God's will in the complexities and ambiguities of human life as it is lived. When we avoid existentially grounding God's word in the lives of people, we make the word ethereal rather than incarnational. It ceases to be born in Bethlehem, tempted in the wilderness, or crucified on Golgotha. Instead, it becomes a platonic ideal.

Plato believed that all human insights were pale reflections of pure "forms" that lie beyond the apprehension of humankind. Qualities such as love, virtue, and justice were eternal ideas that could only be imperfectly understood in this life but communed with forever by the soul in the realm of eternal ideas after death.

A church that offers its theology as a platonic ideal, rather than as incarnational truth, does not offer images of God that transfigure or empower the lives of people, but instead invites Christians to content themselves with metaphysical speculation. In such cases individuals strive to be obedient to otherworldly doctrine while losing the art of personal relationship with God.

Parker Palmer has noted that the church suffers from an improper understanding of transcendence. He suggests that spiritual formation in the lives of contemporary Christians has been stunted because we popularly believe that we can achieve a connection with God only as a result of "upward and outward escape from the realities of self and the world."[1] He offers an alternative understanding: "Transcendence is a breaking-in, a breathing of the spirit of love into the heart of our existence, a literal in-spiration that allows us to regard ourselves and our world with more trust and hope than ever before."[2]

A theology of divorce needs to resist the temptation to label the divorced as estranged from God and confirm that the Spirit of Love is breathing into the hearts of those who suffer from broken marriages. It needs to exchange reflexive judgment through platonic absolutes for the Christlike ability to heal with sensitive understanding. Here the church needs a Christology that intentionally reflects the implications of Jesus' own person-centered theology that provided a compelling, even revolutionary, alternative to the compulsive legalisms of the Pharisees:

> And as he sat at table in his house, many tax collectors and sinners were sitting with Jesus and his disciples; for there were many who followed him. And the scribes and the Pharisees, when they saw that Jesus was eating with sinners and tax collectors, said to his disciples, "Why does Jesus eat and drink with tax collectors and sinners?" And when Jesus heard it, he said to them, "those who are well have no need of a physician, but those who are sick; I came not to call the righteous, but sinners" [based on Matthew 9:10–13].

To all Christians whose marriage has died, the only healing, empowering theology is one that takes account of their pain and touches it with compassion. As Robert Weiss has noted:

> Although no systematic information is available on helping people in crises, unsystematic observation suggests that almost the only useful form of help is support. Support is furnished by a helper (who may or may not be a professional) who is accepted as an ally by the distressed individual.[3]

[103]

In the Christian tradition, supportive allies are those who are able to practice community with others regardless of the labels and stereotypes that invite them to distance themselves from those who the ecclesiastical laws say are lacking in piety. In the Christian tradition it does not matter whether one's neighbor is a tax collector, an adulterer, or a sinner; the Christian is to eat and drink with them in order to share God's transcending presence. In our own time it does not matter whether one's brother or sister is divorced: Christians are to do their theology through the practicing of community. A decisive theology of divorce, then, rests on the response of relationship with those whose most precious relationship has ended. This response of relationship is not an act of charity, but a mutual enjoyment of companionship. It is characterized, not by the giving of advice or the fixing of pain, but by friendship.

An intriguing symbol for this practicing of community is that of the feast. A theology of divorce is a theology of feeding those who question their self-worth with the nurturing word of God. John Burkhardt has rightly noted that "we need to think 'Jesus' in relation to every meal when community is scattered. Then, perhaps, we will be prepared to celebrate deeply at the eucharist table."[4]

Divorce is a fundamental way in which the community of Christ is scattered in our time. A theology of divorce is one that acts to reconcile the fragmentation of the church that occurs when primary estrangements occur. It therefore holds a feast with the divorced specifically in order to feed the hunger that accompanies the loss of a love. This feast is of two kinds. It is, on the one hand, a eucharistic meal that heals people through the mystical repetition of the Last Supper. This Last Supper, it should be remembered, is a meal that commemorates the intimate connectedness of God and human community before the human community divorces Christ. On the other hand, the meal is a next supper—a meal of bread and fish on the Sea of Tiberias with those who have broken a vow. In both cases the feast recalls the depths of commitment into which we are called by God. And it offers a source from which we can borrow strength to pursue more profound and inclusive community.

We have seen that the church needs to practice a theology of the feast with the divorced in order to offer a healing theology. Now a more fundamental question needs to be asked: Is divorce a sin?

The church historically has suggested that this is the case, and divorced Christians have clearly struggled with this judgment in order to overcome feelings of sinfulness. But such realities are different from suggesting that divorce is inherently sinful. In this regard a critical distinction needs to be made by the church which suggests that while divorce has much of sin in it, the event itself is not necessarily sinful. This contention can be evidenced in particular circumstances of divorce. A man who is possessed by a "midlife crisis" and divorces his wife in order to pursue a sexual infatuation with a "more desirable" woman, sins. The sin, in this case, is not the act of divorce, but the more fundamental act of discarding commitments for purposes of self-gratification. In such situations the church needs to search beneath the label of "divorce" in order to perceive the more painful issues that are the sin. A woman who is suffering through such a divorce communicated the deeper issues:

> I am not divorced yet. My divorce will probably be final next month. My husband and I have been separated for one and a half years. It has taken this long to come to the point where I think it is the best thing for both of us.
>
> It was just about two years ago that my husband told me that he wanted to leave and had felt that way for a long time. It was a total shock to me. He agreed to go to marriage counseling, but it didn't help much, as he did not have the desire to work on the marriage. His attachment was to another woman whom

he had been friends with at work. For me, all the heart and soul had been taken out of the marriage. He then got sick with an attack of appendicitis and I "nursed" him through that. It seemed like things were a little better. Then, after he recovered, he went back for counseling, and the therapist gave him the courage to stand up and tell me how he had been having an affair for a long time and was going to leave. I felt anger, hurt, pain, and sadness, like I wasn't given a chance to fix things.

To suggest to this woman that her divorce is a sin is unjust. It is to blame the victim rather than to extend compassion. The church needs to consider that many divorces are the consequence of "the heart and soul being taken out of a marriage," and that people who are involved in such dead relationships may be making a positive decision when they choose to end them.

This possibility becomes even more apparent when we consider issues of abuse. Does a woman who chooses to divorce a husband who physically batters her commit a sin, or does she liberate herself from a sinful relationship? In such a situation the cliché that divorce is a sin is bad theology precisely because it is not grounded in the situation that it is seeking to inform. Far from condemning the wife who files for divorce from a battering husband, God blesses and seeks to comfort her. A woman wrote about the difficulties she had in feeling she had a right to end a destructive marriage:

I was twenty years old when I married. I married a man who had had a previous marriage that lasted two years. He was a wife abuser and had the potential of becoming a child abuser. He was a twenty-two-year-old alcoholic. I thought I could help and turn his life around. My Christian upbringing gave me what I thought was no alternative but to help this man. It became the same old story about being unable completely to change someone. I'm not sure I've ever completely gotten over the hurt that takes place from a divorce. It gave me a very poor self-concept as well as insecurity with jobs and friends. I felt everyone looked at me as a "divorcee," which in this community was considered an outcast.

Superficial theologizing tacitly perpetuates such experiences because it affiliates sin with categories instead of with the complexity and paradox of human life. Superficial theologizing suggests, for instance, that all abortion is a sin, regardless of the context, and that all premarital sex is inherently an abomination and all postmarital sex necessarily blessed. When this style of superficial theology is applied to the issue of divorce, situations such as the following emerge:

> Before making the decision to leave, I was told by my parents that marriage is binding; there is no such thing as divorce to God. My pastor encouraged me to stay with the marriage and make the best of it. I felt marriage needed two people to make it work, and my husband had no interest in working on it. I kept thinking that God couldn't blame me for the failure totally and that this couldn't be how God meant marriage to be. I felt that marriage was my hell. I felt I was a failure totally as a person. My mother made it perfectly clear that to even consider marriage again, which she felt was inevitable because I was so young, was wrong. She said that it was adultery and unacceptable to God, her, and the community.
>
> When I moved back home I did not feel at all acceptable to the community or the members of the church. They felt sorry for me, but I did wrong—no forgiving.

Sin, however, cannot adequately be explained or understood in categorical ways. Such an approach inevitably does violence to the integrity of individual faith. In its desire to set forth universal, inspired truths, this style of theology reduces the mystery of forgiveness to parochial proportions, and therefore sacrifices the wildness of God's grace for the tameness of ecclesiastical law.

A deep theology, by contrast, counteracts such categories

and stereotypes. In the context of divorce, it is a theology that refrains from considering sin in the wholesale sense and instead addresses it in the particular lives of people, as Jesus did with the woman at the well. When we focus on divorce through this kind of theologizing, we are far less prone to make knee-jerk judgments and far more prepared to understand the people who are involved in the drama. And we often discover, to our surprise, that an action or decision we think is contradictory to the will of God is perceived by a divorcing man or woman as a healthy decision. A woman shared the way in which a faith retreat led her to perceive the dishonesty of her marriage and the need for divorce as an act of faith.

> My first recognition of this reality came when I was at a retreat with Ruth Carter Stapleton. There was a meditation on the woman at the well, and I knew I was that woman in some ways—not that I had five husbands, but that I had no husband. It took me about three years after that recognition to actually do what I needed to do.

I am not trying to romanticize or legitimate all divorce, but I am suggesting that it is essential for churches to look at divorce in a person-centered manner if a compassionate ministry is to be provided to the divorced. This means that we cannot presume to call divorce a sin until we touch the people involved and empathize with their life space.

Eleanor Scott Meyers has suggested that the church not only needs to understand the divorced, but also to "revere" them. This is an important contention because it leads us to reflect on the reasons we have been so ill at ease with the divorced and so aloof from their life experience.

Our discomfort with the divorced is a function of our fear about the unresolved vulnerability in our own relationships. The divorced frighten us because they remind us of the fragile nature of covenant, love, and commitment. In this regard the divorced are treated as the dying were once treated. Fifteen years ago the church—like the culture-at-large—was frightened of death, and its members avoided the dying. The pain of the dying made us so uncomfortable that we evaded the feelings involved. Because we didn't confront our fears we repressed them and exiled the dying to places set apart. We asked others to minister to them in our name and contented ourselves with discipleship in the land of the living.

With the aid of the Kübler-Ross research on the stages of death and dying, the church gradually came to see that it could encourage its people to explore death openly. Christians suddenly began sharing their experiences, struggles, and fears. In this sharing we came to see the possibility of opening the community to a group of people we had been treating as outcasts. As we extended compassion and understanding to the dying, we discovered that the historic estrangement came, not from the dying, but from the living who were afraid of the feelings that were catalyzed by their contact with death.

This same dynamic now holds sway with the divorced. We fully understand that we distanced ourselves from the dying because we were afraid of death, but we have not yet fully accepted that we avoid the divorced because of our anxiety of separation, loneliness, and broken love.

The church needs to teach that divorce, like death, is part of the human condition. We need to perceive that each of us, in varying measure, is divorced from someone and from parts of the natural world. This state of divorcedness occurs on at least four levels.

More than a century ago Chief Seattle noted that the natural order is part of our family with which we must keep faithful relationship if we wish to live in harmony with life.

> The white man's dead forget the country of their birth when they go to walk among the stars. Our dead never forget this beautiful earth, for it is the mother of the red man. We are a

[109]

part of the earth and it is part of us. The perfumed flowers are our sisters; the deer, the horse, the great eagle, these are our brothers. The rocky crests, the juices of the meadows, the body heat of the pony and man—all belong to the same family. . . . You must teach your children that the ground beneath their feet is the ashes of our grandfathers. So that they will respect the land, tell your children that the earth is rich with the lives of our kin. Teach your children what we have taught our children, that the earth is our mother. Whatever befalls the earth befalls the sons of earth. This we know. The earth does not belong to man; man belongs to the earth. All things are connected like blood which unites one family. Man did not weave the web of life, he is merely a strand in it. Whatever he does to the web, he does to himself.[5]

Yet we are divorced from the ecosystem. Our marriage to the natural order has died. We have turned the rain to vinegar and filled the aquifer with chemicals. We have cut and carved the land with a callous ruthlessness. The beasts of the field, the birds of the air, and the creatures of the sea continue to wink out like dying stars. Each day a species becomes extinct. Who dares claim that we are faithfully wed to the web of life?

We are divorced from friends, acquaintances, and colleagues. Those who we feel betrayed us are often cut off. Colleagues with whom we compete or disagree are avoided and gossiped about. Parents and siblings who do not understand our life-style are related to in a polite but distant way. Children are "disowned." In our modern culture, relationships are disposable. We seek short-term involvements and allow them to wither as our interests or location change.

Thus we also are divorced from community. We live in a culture of frightening individualism. We pursue self-sufficiency far more frequently than relationship and flee into the world to lose ourselves in things and activities. We hope that hot tubs, health spas, and other accoutrements of the good life will soothe our restless spirits. But what is most lacking in our lives is people—friends in whom to confide and with whom to play. We need to recognize the extent to which our way of life divorces us from community, and we need to practice the discipline of yearning for a return to intimate relationship with others. Henri Nouwen has suggested that we must remember friendships in order to participate in community. In this remembering, our estrangements and loneliness have the potential of being transposed into new or renewed relationship:

> When we remember each other with love we evoke each other's spirit and so enter into a new intimacy, a spiritual union with each other. At the same time, however, the loving memory always makes us desire to be in touch again, to see each other anew, to return to the shared life where the newly found spirit can become more concretely expressed and more deeply imbedded in the mutuality of love.[6]

A painful past mitigates against loving memory. When one feels rejected or unreceived it is difficult to return to the shared life. Old wounds in places left behind sometimes haunt one more than the smiles of old friends can ever heal, and one finds oneself unwilling or unable to reach back into this period of suffering in order to practice relationship.

We have all fled from oppressive, painful spaces that jarred our self-worth to the bone and erased the meaning of life from our hearts. It is not always wrong to leave a land of death. Sometimes one is called to shake the dust from one's sandals or to leave the dead to bury their dead. What is most tragic about the decision to leave is not a search for a promised land, but our propensity to leave behind the loves of that earlier time and place because they remind us too intimately of the pain we experienced there.

We are divorced not only from friends we have left in the painful places of our past, but also from strangers in the present. It is a cynical, angry time—one in which we are invited to withdraw from the volatile uncertainties of life rather than expose ourselves to ideals. We are encouraged to gainsay our own material survival rather than to promote the common good. We are afraid that we will be victimized by those who prey on the innocent if we expose ourselves too deeply to life. So it is that we withdraw into exclusive enclaves and lose the ability to touch or see that spark of God within every person. We feel sorry for the beaten and robbed victims on the Jericho Road but not enough to stop.

Finally, we must consider the ways in which we divorce ourselves from God. Despite our best intentions, we live fleetingly in spiritual relationship. At many points we withdraw from the community of the church and from the bread and wine. We claim God as the greatest love of our lives but live as if we had no ultimate loyalties. When things are going well we believe that we can take care of ourselves and withdraw from a life of prayer. When God fails to rescue us from moments of tragedy and brokenness, we become angry and disillusioned.

So it is that we are all implicated in divorce. We cannot lay the blame of broken vows on a particular group. Rather, we need to interpret the reality of divorce in its complexity. If we can do this, we will discover a new capacity to respect the pain entailed in broken relationships. Estrangement surrounds us, not only in our married lives, but also in other relationships that connect creation. It takes courage to face this fragmenting of existence, and the capacity to be courageous is a function of the heart.

Hearts must be warmed before the pain of broken relationships can be confronted honestly and healed. The process of heart-warming has to do with offering love before judgment and assurance of pardon before confession. The parable of the prodigal son is instructive in this regard. The prodigal son takes his inheritance and divorces himself from his family in order to experience the world. He soon squanders his money and is reduced to utter poverty. So desperate is his plight that he must eat with the pigs in a barnyard. In desperation he returns home, prepared to confess his failure and throw himself on his father's mercy. The father welcomes the son joyfully. The older brother, however, is resentful, feeling that no thanksgiving should occur in response to such irresponsible behavior.

In too many cases the church has welcomed the divorced like the resentful older brother. We have not always felt free to hold a feast for the one who returns after failing to sustain a marriage. Like the older brother, we have asserted that the church should be sharply critical of one who wastes her or his inheritance. If we are to have a feast, let it be for those who have stayed at home and done their work dutifully and well.

But what are we to say about the welcoming father? When the younger son returns in utter shame, the father runs to greet him. As the son attempts to express his feelings of guilt and failure, he is embraced and kissed. Nonetheless, he confesses his sin: "Father, I have sinned against heaven and before you; I am no longer worthy to be called your son [Luke 15:21]." Amazingly, the father has no need for such apologies. He does not twist the thorns of guilt that sit atop the head of his son, or offer him vinegar to drink, or jab a sword of judgment into his side. Instead, he offers love without cost or condition (Luke 15:22–24):

> But the father said to his servants, "Bring quickly the best robe and put it on him; and put a ring on his hand, and shoes on his feet; and bring the fatted calf and kill it, and let us eat and make merry; for this my son was dead, and is alive again; he was lost, and is found.

The implication of this parable is clear. Compassion is more profound than concern about sin, and it is closer to God's ideal of ministry. In terms of the church's ministry with the divorced, people are to be welcomed into new life. The

[113]

church is to feast and make merry, recognizing that there will be time to reflect on sin after the meal has been eaten.

It is the hospitality offered through the feast that gives hurting people the courage to explore their sin and open themselves to healing. When there is no feast, the divorced are left with an individualistic faith that must sustain itself despite the church rather than because of it:

> The church played no part during my divorce. The church was silent and seemed indifferent to my pain and trouble. No one seemed to understand that I was in anguish. If I did not have such a basically strong faith, I would have left the church because it would have been much simpler and less painful.

Feasts that honor those who return home after a divorce create the conditions for hospitality. They demonstrate that we are valued and respected. They give evidence that people care about feeding us. In this space of nurture, we can take stock of the meaning of love in a deeper way:

> I stayed with my conference activities throughout and found a strong pool of love and support in the friends I had made statewide. My faith remained strong throughout the divorce. I've never felt God to be stern and difficult, but understanding and forgiving. It was encouraging for me to realize as I never had before that others have had much worse difficulties and been given the strength to pull through and that I could tap into that source of peace and love and pull through too. I found that as I let love into me, I could better understand other people and situations. As a result of all that happened, I became far less judgmental than I had been and far more ready to hear and believe someone else's story than I was before. Between personal experience and meditation, I came to see that the world is colored in shades of gray. I guess I grew in compassion because I knew that God's love accepted the grays in my own life.

The insights contained in this story are powerful. They suggest that when the church practices compassion, it encourages its people to form a more inclusive theology and to present less rigid doctrine.

The essential task for the church is to neither proclaim nor defend an unchanging theology. Rather, we are called to craft a flexible theology that ignites imaginations and lives with God's resurrecting presence in the world. Ministry with the divorced is not just a matter of responding to people in need. On a deeper level, this ministry pushes and prods the church to worry less about whom to keep out of the church or convict of sin. Such an agenda is the concern of fundamentalist sects. It is the task of the historic church to provide theological alternatives to those who assert that faithfulness is a matter of dogmatic, parochial exclusivity. There is great need to witness to the fact that God works for the renewing of life in ways that continually surpass human expectation. Tom Driver has offered some intriguing comments about the need of the historic church to recommit itself to a theology that is open to such divine surprise in his work *Christ in a Changing World:*

> The churches like to leave basic theological tenets alone while focusing upon specific moral issues. To do so makes a certain conservative sense from a sociological point of view, but it confuses everyone. If God is the same yesterday and today, and if our teaching about God does not change, how can our ethics change? The inconsistency is readily apparent, and the more liberal churches are weakened by it. The fundamentalist-evangelical churches have the advantage of consistency. They maintain that God and the teachings about Him [sic] do not change and neither does Christian morality. "Old time religion," seeking to avoid the complexities of change, has strong appeal. I see North American Christianity strung out between two poles: on the one hand a liberalism devoted to social change while lacking a clear theology of change in God; on the

[115]

other, a conservatism resisting change and thus allied with reactionary political forces.[7]

The church's ministry with the divorced offers us a meaningful opportunity to develop a decisive theology of "change in God," for it challenges us to love more profoundly, to practice hospitality with a group of men and women previous generations have rejected.

Such a theology, moreover, is not "liberal," but profoundly traditional. We need to recall that Jesus' own ministry was one that prioritized the ability to love in new ways so as to bear witness to Driver's notion of a theology of change in God. The essential thrust of Jesus' healing ministry was precisely to challenge people with new images of the ways in which God heals, forgives, and loves. By contrast, the main schools of Judaism during the time of Christ believed that all illness was a result of God's judgment visited on sinful women and men. When Jesus began freely to offer a ministry of healing, in the name of God, those who believed in an unchanging, dogmatic theology rebelled against him and accused him of tampering with the will of God. It is no accident that a statement in the Talmud notes that Jesus was hanged on a tree on the Passover Eve because he practiced sorcery.[8]

Again, the implications of biblical teaching are clear. As Jesus healed the blind and the lame in order to bear witness to new dimensions of God's love in his time, so are we to welcome the divorced into community in order to practice a deeper understanding of God's love in our own time. If we can do this, we will discover that our theology is being directed toward the process of harmonizing with the wild flow of God's love in history rather than trying to tame it with doctrine. As Alfred North Whitehead puts it, it is the task of theology to offer "evolving notions which strike more deeply into the root of reality."[9]

These evolving notions are not just creative flights of fancy.

Theological reflection in the church must be grounded in the ministry and the teaching of Christ. As my colleague Fred Trost suggests, the critical question around which our theological work must orbit is, What would Jesus say?

Jesus did not say a great deal about divorce. His comments on divorce, in fact, are contained within ten short verses that originate in the Gospel of Mark (10:2–12) and are retranslated in Matthew. In both accounts the Pharisees test Jesus with a question about divorce: "Is it lawful for a man to divorce his wife?" In response, Jesus notes that although the Mosaic law permits divorce, there is a deeper spiritual issue to be considered. The Marcan text reads:

> And Pharisees came up [while Jesus was teaching] and in order to test him asked, "Is it lawful for a man to divorce his wife?" [Jesus] answered them, "What did Moses command you?" They said, "Moses allowed a man to write a certificate of divorce, and to put her away." But Jesus said to them, "For your hardness of heart [Moses] wrote you this commandment. But from the beginning of creation, 'God made them male and female.' 'For this reason a man shall leave his father and mother and be joined to his wife, and the two shall become one flesh.' So they are no longer two but one flesh. What therefore God has joined together, let not man put asunder. And in the house the disciples asked him again about this matter. And he said to them, "Whoever divorces his wife and marries another, commits adultery against her; and if she divorces her husband and marries another, she commits adultery.

Jesus offers three specific teachings about marriage and divorce in this passage. First, he teaches that marriage is a profound spiritual state that weaves together two persons into "one flesh" (10:8).

Second, he calls the teachers of the law to recognize that this profound spiritual state deserves respect. Marriage is not merely a social contract to be dissolved whenever a more desirable man or woman comes along. Rather, marriage is an incarnation of God's desire for a creation that can lose itself in love. Teachers of the faith are not to overlook this spiritual dimension of marriage by encouraging or rubber-stamping divorces with the seal of Mosaic law. Therefore, Jesus warns: "What God has joined together let no one put asunder" (10:9).

Third, and most critical, Jesus tells his disciples that divorce for the sake of remarriage is a form of adultery. The text reads: "Whoever divorces his wife and marries another, commits adultery against her [10:11]." This passage has been analyzed to suggest that all remarriage is a form of adultery and divorce a sin against God. But this is not what the passage says. A careful reading of the text reveals that all divorce is not condemned by Christ. Rather, he suggests that it is a violation of the vows of marriage to discard one's spouse *in order to* marry another. The emphasis is on challenging the mechanical nature of divorce and the casual use of the Mosaic Law to defend it. As *The Interpreter's Bible* points out:

> But there is something else far more important to remember—Jesus himself. He is often the tragically forgotten man in all the legalistic discussions of marriage and divorce. As stressed above, we mangle Jesus out of his true shape when we make him a new legalist, a new chief of the scribes, laying down inflexible codes. . . . We must remember his boundless sympathy with people. With that in mind, when the spiritual conception of marriage is made impossible, when brutality and cruelty put a blight on life, when the future possibilities and character of children hang in the balance, then to make Jesus the inflexible legalist is to distort beyond recognition this image of the Son of Man who lives and speaks in the Gospels.[10]

Jesus' teaching about divorce, then, is this: He asserts that ecclesiastical law must not be used to justify the pain of broken relationships. Rather, the faith must remind people of the spiritual dimensions of marriage so that the sin of exploitative divorce can be identified and the grief of necessary divorce healed.

[118]

Daniel Schmiechen, a United Church of Christ pastor, rightly notes that healing from the pain of life depends on the ability of wounded men and women to turn it over to God. "The only way to heal a broken heart is by turning the pain back to God. If God can use our ambition, God can also use our pain." If this be true, then the church's ministry with the divorced significantly depends on our ability to create learning experiences through which to discover how God can use our pain. In essence, these learning experiences are opportunities through which a ministry of forgiveness occurs on three levels: forgiveness of self, forgiveness of others, and God's forgiveness of us:

> The thing that was very helpful to me was the realization that at some point, everything that happened which I considered bad or wrong had to be forgiven. I knew that my faith would make it possible to forgive anything and that I had to forgive everything or I would wake up five years from now and find that I was so bitter and hateful that anger and resentment were controlling my every step.

The blessing that forgiveness has to offer is lightness; the buoyant feeling that comes when we are no longer burdened by guilt and anger. Guilt and anger are dead weight on the human spirit. So heavy are these feelings that we have to expend all the energy of the present in order to carry the pain of the past.

Forgiveness takes away this dead weight by resolving the past. It does not erase what has been but puts it in perspective. Forgiven people have scars, but they also have resolved feelings of pity. They have suffered, but the pain of the past is not the focal point of their lives.

Authentic forgiveness gives us the knowledge that we are entitled to a whole life. It is liberation from the temptation of hiding from shamefulness in our past or compulsively apologizing for mistakes that we have made. Authentic for-

[119]

giveness is the grace that allows us to be who we are, with a radical appreciation of the ambiguity such being entails. It falls to the church to be a community of hope that binds up wounds. It is our ministry to love those who mourn. It is servanthood to show suffering people how God can use their pain.

We are disciples who are to meet women at the well and give them living water. We are people of faith who are to greet men at the seashore and feed them with bread and fish at dawn. Let the Pharisees worry about whether divorce is a sin. Let them assign blame and perfect the pointing of the finger. As for me, I will struggle to speak of resurrection in the midst of those who, like myself, have broken friendships and have failed to honor marriage vows. Perhaps in this small way I will be led to open my own heart to new beginnings.

Notes

CHAPTER ONE. **Of Death and Flights of Freedom**

1. Irene Claremont de Castillejo, *Knowing Woman* (New York: Harper & Row, 1973), p. 12.
2. George Vukelich, "To See Anew," *Isthmus,* December 28, 1984, p. 28.
3. C.S. Lewis, *A Grief Observed* (New York: Seabury Press, 1961).
4. Abigail Trafford, *Crazy Time: Surviving Divorce* (New York: Bantam Books, 1982), p. 43.
5. Matthew McKay, Peter Rogers, Joan Blades, Richard Gosse, *The Divorce Book* (Oakland, Calif.: New Harbinger Publications, 1984), pp. 19–35.
6. Marilyn Adams, "Kids Aren't Broken by the Breakup," *USA Today,* December 20, 1984.
7. Alice Walker, *In Search of Our Mother's Gardens* (New York: Harcourt Brace Jovanovich, 1983), p. 143.

CHAPTER TWO. **Of Judgment and Grace**

1. Ambrose, *Of Paradise (de Paradiso),* in *The Theology of Marriage: The Historical Development of Christian Attitudes Toward Sex & Sanctity in Marriage,* trans. Joseph E. Kerns (New York: Sheed & Ward, 1964), p. 113. Copyright © 1964, Sheed & Ward, Inc. Reprinted with permission of Andrews, McMeel, and Parker. All rights reserved.

2. Tertullian, Ad Uxorem, in ibid., p. 101.

3. Ambrosiaster, in 1 Corinthians 7:27, in ibid., p. 102.

4. Jerome, *De Perpet,* in ibid., p. 103.

5. Augustine, de Bono Conj., in ibid.

6. The Council of Trent, as presented in Enchiridion Symbolorum, by Denzinger, Bunnwart, in ibid., p. 160.

7. Robert Rainey, *The Ancient Catholic Church* (New York: Charles Scribner's Sons, 1902), pp. 223–24.

8. Ibid., p. 223.

9. Clement of Alexandria, *Stromata,* from Patrologia Graeca, by Migne, in *Theology of Marriage,* op. cit., p. 205.

10. Fulgentius of Ruspe, from Patrologia Latina, in ibid., pp. 207–08.

11. Gobel, Bertholds Predigten, 1905, p. 282, cited in ibid., p. 209.

12. Kerns, in ibid., pp. 210–11.

13. Luis De la Puente, De Christiani Hominis Perfectione, Cologne, in ibid., p. 226.

14. Francis de Sales, *Oevvres Completes,* ed. Albanel et Martin, in ibid., p. 218.

15. Masillon, Careme, *Works,* in ibid., p. 218.

16. Kerns, in ibid., p. 218.

17. James Nelson, *Embodiment: An Approach to Sexuality and Christian Theology* (Minneapolis: Augsburg Press, 1978), p. 55.

18. Ibid., p. 56.

19. Roland Bainton, *The Reformation of the Sixteenth Century* (Boston: Beacon Press, 1952), p. 259.

20. Ibid., p. 260.

21. Philip Greven, *The Protestant Temperament: Patterns of Child-Rearing, Religious Experience, and the Self in Early America* (New York: Alfred Knopf, 1977), p. 106.

22. Ibid.

23. Ibid., p. 107.

24. Ibid.

25. Ibid., p. 188.

26. Shulamith Firestone, *The Dialectic of Sex: The Case for Feminist Revolution* (New York: William Morrow, 1970), p. 18.

27. Greven, *The Protestant Temperament*, op. cit., pp. 142–43.

28. Max Lerner; *America as a Civilization*, vol. 2, *Culture and Personality* (New York: Simon & Schuster, 1957), p. 598.

29. Sandra Brown, "Clergy, Divorce, and Remarriage," *Pastoral Psychology* 30 (Spring 1982):187–97.

30. Abraham Heschel, *A Passion for Truth* (New York: Farrar, Straus & Giroux, 1973), p. 265.

31. Henri Nouwen, *The Genesee Diary* (New York: Doubleday, 1981), p. 143.

32. Lewis Rambo, *The Divorcing Christian* (Nashville: Abingdon Press, 1983), p. 23.

33. Myrna and Robert Kysar, *The Assundered: Biblical Teachings on Divorce and Remarriage* (Atlanta: John Knox Press, 1978), p. 85.

34. Richard Morgan, "Any Balm in Gilead for Divorced Clergy?" *Christian Ministry* 13 (May 1982):24–28.

35. Edward Pfnausch, "The Adaption of the Tribunal," in *Divorce Ministry and the Marriage Tribunal*, ed. James Young (New York: Paulist Press, 1982), p. 20.

36. Charles Kindregan, *A Theology of Marriage: A Doctrinal, Moral, and Legal Study* (Milwaukee: Bruce Co., 1967), pp. 146–47.

37. Leigh Jordahl, "On Clerical Divorce," *Dialog* 14 (1975): 223–25.

38. Leigh Jordahl, "Another Word on Clerical Divorce and Remarriage," *Dialog* 15 (Summer 1976):222–23.

CHAPTER THREE. **Of Samaritans and Slaves' Ears**

1. Clark Moustakas, *Loneliness and Love* (Englewood Cliffs, NJ: Prentice-Hall, 1972), p. 62.

2. Thomas Dicken, "The Mark of a Christian," *Faith at Work*, May/June 1979, p. 35.

CHAPTER FOUR. **Of Sanctuaries and Inns Without Rooms**

1. *Webster's New Collegiate Dictionary*, 8th ed. (Springfield, MA: G. & C. Merriam Co., 1981).
2. Parker Palmer, *To Know as We Are Known* (New York: Harper & Row, 1983), p. 59.
3. Thomas Merton, *The Silent Life* (New York: Farrar, Straus, & Giroux, 1957), p. 6.

CHAPTER FIVE. **"Go and Sin No More"**

1. Parker Palmer, *To Know as We Are Known* (New York: Harper & Row, 1983), p. 13.
2. Ibid.
3. In Kathleen Kircher, "The Shape of Divorce Ministry Today," from *Divorce Ministry and the Marriage Tribunal* (New York: Paulist Press, 1982), p. 3.
4. John Burkhardt, from an unpublished lecture, "Becoming Christian," delivered at St. Benedict's Center, Madison, WI, Lent, 1984.
5. Chief Seattle, "How Can You Buy or Sell the Sky." Excerpt of an address given in 1854 to an assembly of Indian tribes preparing to sign treaties. *A.D.*, May 1980, pp. 30–31.
6. Henri J.M. Nouwen, *The Living Reminder: Service and Prayer in Memory of Jesus Christ* (New York, Seabury Press, 1981), p. 41.
7. Tom Driver, *Christ in a Changing World: Toward an Ethical Christology* (New York: Crossroad, 1981), p. 13.
8. Morton Kelsey, *Healing and Christianity* (New York: Harper & Row, 1973), p. 41.
9. Alfred North Whitehead, *Religion in the Making* (New York: Macmillan, 1926), p. 127.
10. The Interpreter's Bible, vol. 7 (Nashville: Abingdon Press, 1951), p. 798.